Library Services for Career Planning, Job Searching, and Employment Opportunities

Forthcoming topics in *The Reference Librarian* series:

• The Reference Librarian and Implications of Mediation, Number 37

Published:

Library Services for Career Planning, Job Searching, and Employment Opportunities has also been published as *The Reference Librarian*, Number 36, 1992.

The Haworth Press, Inc., 10 Alice Street, Binghamton, NY 13904-1580 USA.

Library of Congress Cataloging-in-Publication Data

Library services for career planning, job searching, and employment opportunities / Byron Anderson, editor.
     p. cm.
    "Has also been published as the Reference librarian, number 36, 1992" – Verso t.p.
    Includes bibliographical references.
    ISBN 1-56024-303-1 (acid free paper)
    1. Libraries and the unemployed. 2. Vocational guidance – Information services. 3. Career education – Information services. 4. Job vacancies – Information services. 5. Reference services (Libraries) I. Anderson, Byron.
Z711.92.U53L54 1992
020'.23 – dc20
                                          92-11277
                                             CIP

Library Services for Career Planning, Job Searching, and Employment Opportunities

Edited by
Byron Anderson

The Haworth Press, Inc.
New York • London • Norwood (Australia)

Library Services
for Career Planning, Job Searching,
and Employment Opportunities

CONTENTS

An Evaluation of the Resume Content Recommendations of Resume Writing Books 153
Barbara E. Weeg

Career Resources in Library Collections 173
Marilyn Searson Lary

ABOUT THE EDITOR

Byron Anderson, MLS, is Assistant Professor at the University Libraries at Northern Illinois University in DeKalb. He is also Coordinator of Computer Access Services which includes both fee-based searching and end-user training in the libraries' online catalog, CD-ROMS, and public OCLC systems. In addition, Mr. Anderson coordinates the libraries' Career Information Services. His research interest in this area has led to the publication of several articles on the topic of career information and libraries.

Introduction:
Expansion of Career
and Job Information Services

Byron Anderson

THEMES FOR THE 1990s

This is the first time known to this author that a publication like this has been devoted entirely to the topic of careers, jobs and libraries. This is surprising considering the degree to which most libraries are involved with providing career and job information, let alone the extent and popularity of career and job material. If anything, this publication is long overdue. The information in this publication will provide the ways and means for libraries to maintain, or moreover, to enhance their career and job information services. The ideas, sources and conclusions presented here emphasize the necessity of career and job information services in the 1990s.

For years, libraries have maintained some degree of current career and job information, whether it be through traditional vocational guidance literature or more indirectly through out-of-town newspapers and telephone books. Beginning in the late 1970s, the W. K. Kellogg Foundation recognized a job information need, and this eventually lead to the funding of Educational Information Centers (EICs) in public libraries. Programs established under these grants allowed career/job services in public libraries to make great strides. The development of career and job services in libraries continued to grow during the 1980s as economic conditions caused wide fluctuations in the labor market. It now appears as libraries embark upon the 1990s, that delivery of career and job information will be one of the growth areas for library service. The enhance-

1

ment and provision of this service could lead the library to be thought of as a career and job information resource in the community. The following are themes weaved through the chapters which include different types of library settings, as well as non-librarian perspectives. The themes capture much of the present picture of careers, jobs and libraries.

Theme: The economy and labor market is no longer stabilized; there is a continual state of change in job turnover and new career opportunities.

Theme: Libraries should not wait for an economic downturn or rising unemployment to establish or strengthen their career and job services. There is a lifelong need for career and job information.

Theme: Most every library has some career and job information available, but the sources are generally disbursed throughout the collection. Once found, patrons do not know how to use them effectively in a career plan or job search.

Theme: Libraries are not the only career/job service providers, but librarians are professional information providers who are able to locate and retrieve needed materials for one's career or job search, and provide assistance in their use. Librarians will often know of useful sources unknown to other professional service providers.

Theme: Libraries can expand services by networking with other career/job service providers in the community. In fact, given the limitation of resources, it is essential to network.

Theme: Marketing of the library's career/job services is necessary. Many potential users are unaware of these services in libraries, and an expansion of services without marketing will not expand the user base.

SETTING THE STAGE

The "one life, one job" previously the norm is now the exception. Most employed persons will experience three to four different careers during his or her lifetime, and various job positions within each career area. Each career plan and job search will require new information. This makes career and job information a lifelong need, and ties it closely to lifelong learning. Moreover, the workforce has changed, and is now made up of more single-parent families, ethnic and racial minorities, older adults, and the physically challenged. Each has its own information and service needs.

Developing a career plan or launching a job search is usually a complex process, and requires an examination of individual goals, values, workplace issues, and personal constraints, as well as information about occupations, career ladders, options, and positions available. This process is often concurrent with emotional strains placed on the individual going through this process. An individual must not only figure out what to do with their life, but also secure a position that they find meaningful. These processes are among the most challenging in all of life. Where and how does one begin? Many individuals lack the skills necessary to proceed with a meaningful career or job search.

As an extension of its services, libraries must stay attuned to today's career and job information needs. Librarians must no longer be content with merely directing an individual to an occupational literature section, sample resumes, or job postings board. In short, career and job information services in libraries should no longer be a marginal service. These articles will show how to provide effective service, often within budget constraints.

HELP FOR LIBRARIES

There is help available for librarians looking to establish new career and job services, or strengthen existing services. First, efforts such as the information presented in this publication, along with other useful material, will assist in developing both awareness and ideas. A review of the literature is always a good starting point, and this publication conveniently brings together under one cover a lot of relevant information. The information presented will be useful for most of the 1990s when examining careers, jobs and libraries, and will at least initially upon its publication present many new and updated sources, so crucial a factor in this area.

Second, there is, at least for public librarians, a place to gather within the structure of the American Library Association. The Public Library Association's Adult Lifelong Learning Section has a committee, Job and Career Information Services. The charge of this committee is, in part:

- To encourage the development of job and career information services in public libraries.
- To provide continuing education and information about these services to the library community.
- To act as a liaison with other agencies providing related services.
- To develop guidelines for the provision of job and career information services by public libraries.

This active committee has many fine dedicated librarians sincerely intent on providing quality career and job services. Their conference programs are well attended and well received. The committee is currently developing as of this writing a manual designed to help libraries take the first step in establishing or strengthening career and job services. This manual will, among other things, evaluate services, suggest strategies, tell where and how librarians can train for these services, and provide testimonials from individuals who have received help from these services. The manual is expected to be available by the summer of 1992.

Third, the American Library Association has available a number of materials to assist libraries in developing their career and job information services. Foremost is the video presentation, "Make a Living/Make a Life." This 15-minute video is primarily a marketing tool to assist libraries in gaining community support. Its goal is to change perceptions of what libraries can do. It can be used with many groups–civic, religious, board of trustees, a library staff reluctant to provide the service, or those involved with a job search. The video ($49.95) is accompanied by a job poster ($4), job pamphlet (100/$24), and a job tip sheet ($2), all available from ALA Video/Graphics, 50 E. Huron St., Chicago, IL 60611, 1-800-545-2433.

Finally, if libraries look to the community, including a college or university community, networking assistance can be established. This publication is replete with networking examples. A career plan or job search is a complex process which requires a variety of resources; rarely will one organization have all of the resources needed.

OTHER ISSUES

Editing this publication has been a real growth experience, one that has held my interest throughout. In bringing this together, I was fortunate to find dedicated individuals who were willing to share their ideas with a wider audience. I am most indebted to the authors of this publication. I would also like to extend special thanks to Bill Katz. In review of my original proposal of the topic, he recognized the theme as unique and worthy of publication. I owe him a great debt of gratitude for his encouragement and insistence on one overriding principle, "as long as quality is king." I have striven for this premise, and can only hope that I'm in the ballpark.

Months back, in reaching out to potential authors for proposals, I was successful in striking a balance by receiving manuscripts from librarians in public, academic and special library settings, as well as from non-librarian professionals in the career/job service areas. I have arranged the chapters in this publication in such a way as to be read from the approach of library experiences in general, rather than categorical sections, such as academic, public, and special libraries. The content of each chapter will likely relate some relevant or new information which will be of use to readers.

I was unsuccessful in receiving manuscripts on career and job services in rural library settings, or career services in school libraries. While one arrived that addressed the employment needs of disabled persons, I would have welcomed receiving others discussing the needs of special groups, for instance, racial and ethnic minorities, single-parent households, or older adult workers. These are important pieces in the full picture of careers, jobs and libraries.

The chapters in this publication lay a foundation upon which one can surmise research needs and direction. From my perspective, research is needed in developing a better understanding of how career or job seekers view libraries, utilize career and job information, and as a result, how librarians can provide better reference service. In addition, further work is needed on understanding and orienting the reference interview to the career or job seeker. Continual research needs to be done on understanding the career/job information needs of specialized sections of the population, such as new immigrant groups or individuals returning to the workforce after a prolonged absence. It would be interesting to know the influence of career literature on a person's career path. Finally, I know of no recent literature discussing policies governing career collections, e.g., is it a disservice to keep older career material in the stacks?

In developing this publication, I learned a great deal about this topic that I did not know, and I hope readers will have a similar experience, especially in deriving their own ideas or conclusions that can be acted upon. At minimum, this publication should raise a reader's awareness of the issues involved with career and job information services in libraries. I welcome correspondence, either as commentary, criticism, or suggestion on this topic or publication, as well as on future projects.

I. CAREERS, JOBS, AND LIBRARIES: AN OVERVIEW

Information Empowers People to Build Careers

Nancy L. Larson
Carole Minor

SUMMARY. A majority of Americans surveyed indicated a need for occupational information and career planning assistance. Career counseling is a process of examining individual needs, goals, values, workplace issues, and personal constraints, as well as information about occupations, career ladders, options and specific employment opportunities, and relating all this information to make decisions about work and other career issues.

Developmental theories of career counseling can be used as a framework for examining theories of career development. Other ways to examine career development are through occupational choices, work adjustment, a combination of choice and adjustment process theories, and decision-making.

Dr. Nancy L. Larson is a student in the Department of Library and Information Science Studies at Northern Illinois University, DeKalb, IL 60115. Dr. Carole Minor is Associate Professor in the Department of Educational Psychology, Counseling, and Special Education at Northern Illinois University and was past president of the National Career Development Association.

7

The role of the librarian is one of facilitating access to the abundance of career information available, and empowering patrons to use this information to make intelligent decisions about not only their careers, but also other areas of their lives as well.

INTRODUCTION

In a recent survey entitled, "National Survey of Working America," conducted for the National Career Development Association by the Gallup Organization, a number of findings emerged regarding career information and assistance needs among Americans. Almost two-thirds of those surveyed would try to get more information about jobs if they could start their lives over again. About one in four (which is equivalent to about 48 million persons) indicated they needed assistance in finding information about jobs. One in four respondents had not used sources of career information such as newspapers, magazines, career information centers or employment agencies. African Americans, Hispanics, and Asian-Pacific Islanders in particular reported a greater need for information about careers and more assistance in finding job information (National Career Development Association, 1990).

Clearly, there is a need for Americans to obtain more information about occupations and career paths. This information becomes more critical as one examines such issues as the increasing numbers of ethnic minorities (Hughes and Smith, 1987), women (Farmer, 1985), and the physically challenged (Marks and Lewis, 1983), who are members of traditionally underserved populations in terms of career planning, but who are entering the workforce in ever-increasing numbers. Additional issues include the effects of work on the family, dual career couples (Wilcox-Matthew and Minor, 1989), the complexity of career planning, and the increasing demands for change on American workers as society moves into the 21st century.

Increasingly, libraries can play an important role in providing information critical to so many people in their communities. It is useful to look at the career counseling process and the theory underlying it to determine how this information might best be used.

WHAT IS CAREER COUNSELING?

Career counseling is a process of examining individual needs, goals, values, workplace issues and personal constraints as well as information about occupations, career ladders, options and specific employment opportunities, and relating all this information to make decisions about work and other career issues.

Examination of career counseling theories gives greater understanding about the practical aspects of career development and planning. What follows is a brief overview of career counseling theories. For more information, two important resources on career counseling theory and practice are *Career Choice and Development*, by Duane Brown and Linda Brooks (1987), and *Adult Career Development*, edited by Zandy Leibowitz and Daniel Lea (1986). It is useful to consider career development as a continuous process, consisting of career choice and career adjustment, and to focus on either the content or process of career choice and adjustment (Minor, 1986).

DEVELOPMENTAL THEORIES

Developmental theories are often used as a framework when examining other theories of career development, and include the work of theorists such as Donald Super and Dalton, Thompson and Price.

Super (1953, 1976) perceived career development as a process, rather than a one-time event. People are different, and their personalities qualify them for a number of occupations. The process of change can be summarized as a cycle of growth, exploration, establishment, maintenance, and decline. This process can occur repeatedly, especially during times of transition or instability in an individual's life. Additionally, people perform different roles at different times in their life.

Although the Dalton, Thompson and Price (1977) model is somewhat limited, it illustrates career development in professional organizations by dividing progression in the organization into four stages. First, the person is newly-hired and begins to learn about the organization and perform routine tasks. The psychological issue here is dependence. The second task is learning responsibility for projects from start to finish, and being viewed as a colleague. The third stage involves taking responsibility for the work of others, while the final stage means taking responsibility for policymaking and the direction of the organization–a stage few individuals reach.

The developmental framework identifies career development as a process, rather than an isolated event. Job changes are a part of normal development. Everyone will have them periodically during their life. Librarians can provide information as a continuing and changing part of people's lives, with the user identifying job changes and information needs as part of the inevitable transition and flow of life.

CHOICE

Many career theories describe the content of career choice. That is, they predict what occupational choice the individual will make from certain individual characteristics. Examples of such theories are those of John Holland and Helen Astin.

Holland (1973) found that occupational choices could be predicted based upon the personality characteristics of an individual. He devised a typology of six personality types: Realistic, Investigative, Artistic, Social, Enterprising, and Conventional. The personality types of the individual in a particular working environment determine the personality type of that environment. Holland states that individuals seek to work in environments congruent with their own personality types. Holland's typology is the basis of many interest inventories as well as best-sellers such as *What Color Is Your Parachute?*

Astin (1984) describes four constructs for a sociopsychological model of career development: motivation, expectations, sex-role socialization, and the structure of opportunity. These constructs interact to explain career choices. Astin believes that work itself satisfies three basic human needs: survival, pleasure, and contribution to others. Career choices are based upon how various kinds of work satisfy these basic needs. Early socialization and the structure of opportunity interact and affect career choices, particularly for women, while changes in expectations and opportunities lead to changes in career choices and work behavior.

Other factors which influence career decisions include interest and personality patterns. According to Krumboltz (1979), who based ideas on social learning theory, individuals would be more likely to enter occupations with activities for which they have been positively reinforced, rather than punished. Krumboltz identified four categories of influences: (1) genetic endowment and special abilities are inherited qualities the individual is born with that may limit education and occupational preferences. This might include aspects such as intelligence, musical ability, or other traits which may predispose an individual to certain types of learning experiences. (2) Environmental conditions and events, including factors outside the control of the individual such as nature of job opportunities, social policies for selecting workers, and natural or physical events which cannot be modified by an individual. (3) Learning experiences and their reinforcement, such as skills necessary for career planning, obviously influence one's ability to select appropriate occupations. Lastly (4), task approach skills are the interaction between learning experiences, genetic endowment, and environmental influences which all affect how an individual will approach a task or problem, and modification of the outcome due to the interaction of these factors. These four influences help explain the wide variation in individual skills and abilities, and what librarians, and other professionals can do to assist individuals into more productive work lives.

ADJUSTMENT

Work adjustment or job satisfaction has often been ignored by career counselors. Individual abilities and the requirements of the workplace need to mesh, resulting in "satisfactoriness" and the individual needs to be rewarded for his or her efforts ("satisfaction'') (Minor, 1986). Both the individual and the organization have any number of expectations regarding the amount and type of work performed, the responsibility and skill of the person performing the work, recognition and approval for such work, and other expectations. The clearer the expectations, the more likely counselors will be able to identify and assist dissatisfied workers (Morgan, 1980).

CHOICE AND ADJUSTMENT PROCESS THEORY

Tiedeman and O'Hara (1963) described the process of both career choice and adjustment of the individual over time, and consisting of two stages, with several steps within the stages. These stages continue throughout the life of the individual, and describe a natural rhythm of change and adjustment.

The first stage, anticipation, begins with the individual randomly exploring and interacting with the world of work by collecting information and receiving feedback, and incorporating the information. Crystallization occurs when the individual takes the feedback and incorporates it into patterns. Awareness of observation and crystallization result in the individual making tentative choices, and clarification occurs when the person begins to prepare for entry into an occupation.

The second stage is one of implementation, and the first step is one of induction, when the individual first enters a particular field, and learns what is expected in the organization. Finally, there is an integration between the individual and the organization, with satisfaction until the balance changes, and the cycle begins again.

In expanding the choice adjustment process theory, Miller-Tiedeman (1988) believes that each individual's life is a career, and choices must be made about how the person will live his or her life. The goal for the individual is to integrate all aspects of life and become empowered to act on personal dreams and goals. Such a concept encourages self-awareness, communication, and personal responsibility, rather than simply trying to find the one ''right'' job or career.

THE DECISION-MAKING PROCESS

Along with career counseling, counselors attempt to teach clients how to make decisions and take control of their lives. Empowering individuals requires not only large amounts of information, but also self-awareness. In most models of decision-making, career counselors encourage clients to identify a particular problem or issue to resolve, for example, making a career change. Next, strategies are generated for identifying ways to achieve that particular goal. Two important strategies are brainstorming numerous ideas or options, then gathering information about ideas which particularly interest the individual.

Clients can take interest inventories, utilize tools such as the Self-Directed Search, an inventory based upon Holland's theory of types, and other means of self-exploration. What kind of hobbies does the person enjoy? What kinds of experiences in their lives have given them the greatest satisfaction? Self-awareness is incorporated with the factual knowledge obtained elsewhere. As this information is gathered, the client and counselor begin to create action plans for targeting specific industries or companies for possible careers within the company, and ultimately a job which meets the needs of the individual and the company. The goals and strategies change as needed, and information is continuously gathered throughout the process.

ROLE OF THE LIBRARIAN

Librarians can play a critical role in making patrons aware of the large amount of information available on specific occupations, resources for gathering information about particular companies, preparing for the job interview, job clubs, resume writing, and so on.

Although counselors are skilled in counseling, they are sometimes not as skilled in utilizing information available regarding career issues. More adults are using libraries as a career information source for a number of reasons, including availability of information resources, librarians who can facilitate the career planning process, and assistance in examining the role of work in their lives (Durrance, 1991).

In view of the increased demand upon library resources and librarian for career information, the role of the librarian in providing access to information about occupations and career planning becomes more important. In addition, the demand for information goes beyond giving the patron the *Occupational Outlook Handbook* and samples of resumes. What can librarians do, particularly in smaller libraries which do not have many resources?

- Make patrons aware that career information is available. A section of the reference area can be set aside, and career information can be placed near the business reference section. College and vocational training information can be prominently displayed. You do not have to be a career counselor, but rather help the patron become acquainted with what is available.
- Identify self-help tools and books for personal exploration and the career development process. Bolles' (1991) *What Color Is Your Parachute?*, or Chapman's (1987) *How to Make a Thousand Dollars a Minute* are only two examples of books suitable for career guidance. Another valuable tool which combines self-exploration and occupational information are computer-assisted career guidance systems such as SIGI PLUS or DISCOVER.
- Become aware of resources in your area. Community colleges, universities, and social service agencies often have career counseling resources. A vertical or pamphlet file is helpful.
- Make a monetary and practical commitment to locating timely and appropriate career materials. Perhaps a library professional can receive additional training and information about career planning and resources.
- Sponsor a presentation on what resources are available in the library for career planning and development. Actually show patrons what materials are available, and how to use them. An outside speaker might be willing to speak for free or at nominal cost to explain how to conduct a job search or find additional resources.

- Be creative. Reference sources which might not be considered strictly "Career information," such as almanacs, telephone directories, statistical abstracts, and other reference materials can assist patrons in their quest for career information.
- Provide space for Job Clubs or other support groups for those who are seeking employment. Have newspapers and other materials available for the job search.

CONCLUSION

Finding a good job and building one's career are never easy tasks, particularly in changing or uncertain economic times. American workers not only want jobs which meet basic survival needs, but many are also seeking personal satisfaction, to "follow their bliss," rather than punching a timeclock. The role of the librarian is one of facilitating access to the wealth of career information available, and empowering patrons to use this information to make intelligent decisions about not only their careers, but also other areas of their lives as well.

REFERENCES

Astin, H. (1984). "The Meaning of Work in Women's Lives: A Sociopsychological Model of Career Choice and Work Behavior." *The Counseling Psychologist*, 12, 117-126.

Bolles, R. (1991). *What Color Is Your Parachute? A Practical Manual for Job-hunters and Career Changers*. Annual. Berkeley, CA: Ten Speed Press.

Brown, D., and Brooks, L., eds. (1987). *Career Choice and Development*. San Francisco, CA: Jossey-Bass.

Chapman, J. (1987). *How to Make $1000 a Minute: Negotiating Salaries and Raises*. Berkeley, CA: Ten Speed Press.

Dalton, G., Thompson, P. and Price, R. (1977). "Career Stages: A Model of Professional Careers in Organizations." *Organizational Dynamics*, 6, 19-42.

Durrance, J. (1991). "Public Libraries and Career Changers: Insights from Kellogg-funded Sources." *Public Libraries*, 30, (2): 93-100.

Farmer, H. (1985). "Model of Career and Achievement Motivation for Women and Men." *Journal of Counseling Psychology*, 32, 363-390.

Holland, J. (1973). *Making Vocational Choices: A Theory of Careers*. Englewood Cliffs, NJ: Prentice-Hall.

Hughes, A. and Smith B. (1987). "Career Development and the Ethnic Minority. In: Z. Leibowitz and D. Lea, eds., *Adult Career Development: Concepts, Issues and Practices*, pp. 163-170. Alexandria, VA: American Association for Counseling and Development.

Krumboltz, J. (1979). "A Social Learning Theory of Career Decision Making." In: A. Mitchell , G. Jones and J. Krumboltz, eds., *Social Learning and Career Decision Making*, pp. 19-49. Cranston, RI: Carroll Press.

Leibowitz, Z. and Lea, D., eds. (1986). *Adult Career Development: Concepts, Issues and Practices*. Alexandria, VA: American Association for Counseling and Development.

Marks, E. and Lewis A. (1983). *Job Hunting for the Disabled*. New York: Barron's Educational Series, Inc.

Miller-Tiedeman, A. (1988). *Lifecareer: The Quantum Leap into a Process Theory of Career*. Vista, CA: Lifecareer Foundation.

Minor, C. (1986). "Career Development: Theories and Issues." In: A. Leibowitz and D. Lea, eds., *Adult Career Development: Concepts, Issues and Practices*, pp. 17-39. Alexandria, VA: American Association for Counseling and Development.

Morgan, M. A. (1980). *Managing Career Development*. New York: Van Nostrand Reinhold.

National Career Development Association (1990). *National Survey of Working America 1990*. Alexandria, VA: Author.

Super, D. (1953). "A Theory of Vocational Development." *American Psychologist*, 8, 185-190.

Super, D. (1976). *Career Education and the Meaning of Work*. Washington, DC: U. S. Government Printing Office.

Tiedeman, D. V. and O'Hara, R. P. (1963). *Career Development: Choice and Adjustment*. New York: College Entrance Examination Board.

Wilcox-Matthew, L. and Minor, C. (1989). "The Dual Career Couple: Concerns, Benefits, and Counseling Implications." *Journal of Counseling and Development*, 68, 194-198.

Delivering Career and Job Information: A Place for Libraries

Byron Anderson

SUMMARY. Today's labor market has become increasingly complex, and the average career or job seeker has been left stranded. New information is required at every turn. Libraries are in a position to be a prime player in the delivery of career and job sources and services. Before doing so, however, libraries must have key personnel who:

- are knowledgeable of labor market and employment trends;
- develop strong core collections in career and job sources;
- are well versed in accessing information, including various formats and nontraditional sources;
- network with other community career/job resources; and
- market the library's services.

In doing so, libraries have the opportunity to provide much of the information required for a career or job search, and in the process can enhance its reputation within the community.

. . . [I]n an information society all people should have the right to information which can enhance their lives. . . . What is true today is often outdated tomorrow. A good job today may be obsolete next year. To promote economic independence and quality of existence, there is a lifelong need for being informed and up-to-date.

(American Library Association, 1989)

Byron Anderson is the Coordinator for Computer Access Services at the University Libraries, Northern Illinois University in addition to providing for the Libraries' Career Information Services.

Unplanned, random learning is not likely to bring people the information they need to understand the increasingly complex American labor market.

(Wegmann, Chapman and Johnson, 1989)

INTRODUCTION

The complexity of today's labor market is putting the individual career developer or job hunter at a disadvantage. Growth opportunities in new careers and jobs are on the increase, but these in turn require new information and skills. The best places to look for comprehensive job and career resources eludes most people. Where and how does one begin? Libraries unquestionably play a role in this area, but they need to develop a stronger service capacity and reputation for career planners and job seekers. Played well, this role will ideally complement other job/career resources in the community.

COMPREHENSIVE SCOPE

Libraries that try to provide all the information needs for career planners and job seekers, require a lot of resources. Taking a holistic approach, a library would need sources and services that provides information on as many of the following career/job related categories as possible:

Self Identity

- knowledge of self: work values, personality characteristics, psychological traits, and physical constraints;
- knowledge of skills: abilities, spare time activities, and aptitudes;
- exploration of career interests in varied formats and comprehensiveness: pamphlets, articles, books, videos, software programs, etc.

Education/Training

- awareness of different workplace literacy requirements;
- local literary training and GED programs;
- continuing education and training program opportunities;
- choice of major and career implications;
- internship and apprenticeship information;
- volunteer work;
- test guides and preparation for aptitude tests;
- sources of financial aids.

Job Search

- professional organizations and their relationship to careers and jobs;
- company, agency and industry information;
- self employment/entrepreneurship guidance;
- employer identification: public, private, government and non-profit;
- current job listings;
- referral to or networking with job search resources in the community.

Career/Job Preparation

- resumes, cover letters, and interviews;
- salary surveys;
- cost of living comparisons;
- relocation information.

Real world considerations of time, space, budget, administrative commitment, user perception, etc., are all barriers which prevent libraries from developing comprehensive career/job resources, though a few have come close. On a more positive note, there are at least two reasons why libraries may not need to consider providing all the services necessary. First, they can network with other services to extend existing resources. Second, service is driven by need, and the needs of users will vary. Each library must determine user needs first, then examine the possibilities of expanding the job/career sources and services it provides.

Once user needs are determined, development of services and sources must be complemented by librarian knowledge that is able to address broad questions, such as

- What is a career plan and how does one develop a plan to fit his or her needs?
- How do individuals find a match between their interests, skills and background, and labor market needs?
- How can race, gender, age, or disability affect the information and services a career or job hunter needs?
- What does one need to know about herself or himself in order to proceed with a career plan or job search?
- What training or background is required to satisfy the various dimensions of today's workplace literacy, and what options does one have to upgrade one's skills and knowledge?

THE PROBLEM

Finding a career or job for most people is still something they are supposed to figure out on their own (Wegmann, Chapman and Johnson, 1989, p. 243). There can be no doubt about the need for career/job information, let alone the need for clear-marked avenues to deliver this. Libraries are one of the logical service providers for this role, and librarians one of the logical resource persons to enhance the delivery of needed information. Librarians are in the enviable position of being aware of resource material that other career/job professionals may not even be aware of. Career/job seekers should be presented with on-going, well-publicized library services that deliver essential information with a minimum of difficulty. Doing this well is another story.

Career centers in libraries can centralize job/career information and make it more accessible, but most libraries lack the resources and space for such a center. Even when present, some centers fall behind in material currency, accessibility, and service (Jacobson and Palmer, 1991). Such centers require a lot of attention. More often, libraries have a partial career information area or job postings board where users can be directed. To be sure, this may be all smaller libraries can provide. While useful, these areas usually contain only a fraction of the information sought or needed.

Relevant career/job material usually remains dispersed through the collection. Even the main classification sections for "vocational guidance" literature, the Library of Congress HF5382-5383 or Dewey 331.7, useful for browsing, represent only a fraction of the total picture. Not only is career/job material normally dispersed in the library, but also involves different formats: print, microform, audiovisual, newspaper, online, software programs, etc. Few users are able to proceed on their own.

Initially, effective career/job information requires that libraries have up-to-date material. More important though is the awareness and access of this information. Effective delivery of labor market information is dependent on a combination of strong core collections, knowledgeable librarians, library instruction or library-sponsored programs, community networking, and marketing of services. Each of these factors have component parts. For instance, library instruction is made up of signage, guides, reference assistance, and classroom or one-on-one instruction.

EMPLOYMENT TRENDS

Before libraries proceed with establishing or strengthening career/job services, each library should at minimum assign one staff member to the responsibility of developing these services. The responsibilities of this specialist/coordinator/ bibliographer are to become aware of employment trends, changes taking place in the labor market, and how career/job seekers use a collection. The coordinator must also be responsible for keeping other related staff trained.

Keeping abreast of developments in the careers/jobs area is applicable to many library-related functions. For instance, there are strong collection development and service implications in being aware of labor market and employment trends. Consider the following:

1. Career planning is lifelong planning. The "one life, one occupation" is deeply ingrained, yet according to the U. S. Department of Labor, some 12 percent of today's workers change to new careers each year. Over the next decade, job obsolescence will become increasingly commonplace and many people may engage in four or five different careers over a lifetime. Automation of the office and factory, baby boomers hitting their forties, free-trade agreements and the trade imbalance, environmental and energy issues, and legislation are all factors in the destabilized work environment (Gehlen, 1986). Given factors like the above, career/job services in libraries should be available at all times, not just during recessionary or high unemployment periods.

2. Employment projections imply direction for career/job seekers. For instance, service-producing industries will account for almost all of the 18.1 million new jobs expected to be created by the year 2000. These service producing industries–retail trade, health services, and business services–will account for half of this growth (Silvestri and Lukasiewicz, 1989). The driving force behind new productivity gains come from a handful of core technologies, so called because they are the building blocks of new products in virtually every manufacturing and service sector. They include biotechnology, computers, expert systems and artificial intelligence, robotics, lasers and fiber optics, composite materials, and batteries and fuel cells. ("The Shape of Things to Come," 1987). Librarians who can deliver this type of information are providing enhanced and much needed career/job resources.

3. Career and job seekers are engaged in a process, e.g., recently graduated from college and looking for work, re-entering the workforce, looking to upgrade one's skills, or exploring a new career. The library's role in this process is to not only provide the resources sought or needed, but also to know how adults in transition use a library's career/job sources and services (Durrance, 1991).

4. Each career/job change will require new information. Within this framework, librarians should realize that it is not the skills and interests of an individual that counts as much as

their skills in getting a job that count. Libraries can provide job skills training through workshops, videotape presentations and facilities to play the tapes, and referral to other community job skills resources.

5. Career instruction should begin as early as possible in an individual's life. Career development without a path causes an individual to falter in the initial work of building on experiences and interests. Libraries can provide resources which allow individuals, especially young people, to explore career options at various reading and age levels. For adults, material can cover avenues to successful second careers or paths to re-careering.

6. Through classified help wanted ads, only one person in seven will find a job; however, the ads can be used for more than looking for current job openings. Career/job seekers can be instructed to use the ads as an overview of the hiring market in a discipline, an understanding of salary ranges, and current employer expectations (Opritsa, 1986).

7. Today's workforce is becoming more nontraditional, being made up of greater numbers of single parents, minority, older, and impaired individuals. The trends in demography over the next ten years are low birthrate, aging population, high immigration, and rising percentages of racial minorities. By 2000, there will be 34 million Americans over the age of 65, and all racial minorities will account for 28 percent of the population ("The Shape of Things to Come," 1987). This means that a greater variety of resources–materials, workshops, etc., are needed to address the needs of these diverse populations. To meet these needs, consideration should be given to things, such as bilingual materials, day care needs, and providing workshops dealing with employment discrimination.

8. Better-pay jobs now require more literacy and education. There is a shortage of trained workers. The Hudson Institute has estimated that half of the new jobs between now and the year 2000 will require post-high school training (Johnston, 1987). Employers need employees who are, at minimum, literate, have basic mathematics and problem solving abilities, and are able to communicate. At a higher level there is a

demand for employees who are information and computer literate, think critically and creatively, can motivate others, and have a solid grounding in the humanities and social sciences. Individuals need information to determine the investment required to upgrade their skills or education, and what this will mean in the labor market. Libraries can provide this information through materials, referral, and counseling relating to vocational, college, continuing education, and local training opportunities, as well as sources for financial aid. In cojunction with this, materials should be available on occupational outlook and salary surveys.

LABOR MARKET AWARENESS

Professional awareness of the labor market and employment trends is found by reviewing current literature, such as

Boyett, Joseph H. and Henry P. Conn. *Workplace 2000: The Revolution Reshaping American Business.* New York: Dutton, 1991.
Wegmann, Robert G., Robert Chapman and Miriam Johnson. *Work in the New Economy: Careers and Job Seeking into the 21st Century.* Rev. ed. Indianapolis, IN: JIST Works, 1989.
U.S. Department of Labor. Secretary's Commission on Achieving Necessary Skills. *SCANS Report* and *What Work Requires of Schools.* Washington, D.C.: U.S. Government Printing Office, 1991. (Individual copies of these reports are free. Write: Secretary's Commission, 200 Constitution Ave., N.W., Room C 2318, Washington, DC 20210, or call 800-788-SKILL.)

This reading can be regularly supplemented by browsing periodical literature in journals, such as

U. S. Department of Labor. *Occupational Outlook Quarterly.* Washington, D.C.: U. S. Government Printing Office. Quarterly.
Journal of Career Planning and Employment. Bethlehem, PA: College Placement Council, Inc. Quarterly.

High-interest, current periodical literature can be identified in periodical indexes. Particularly effective are a number of InfoTRAC (Information Access Company) or Wilson indexes, for instance, *Business Periodicals Index, Education Index, General Periodicals Index, General Science Index, Humanities Index, Magazine Index, Reader's Guide,* or *Social Sciences Index.* One should begin with the subject headings "Professions" and "Occupations." When present, these headings will index general articles on careers, e.g., "The Top 20 Professions," "A Look at Occupational Employment Trends to the Year 2000," or "21 Careers at a Glance for Would-be Job Jumpers." In addition, the "Professions" heading will often cross-reference with specific occupations, e.g., "Advertising as a Profession," "Pharmacy as a Profession," "Folklorists," or "Social Work as a Profession." Headings on specific careers such as these will lead to current topics within that occupation, e.g., "Continuity and Change in Police Careers," "Job Satisfaction of Journalist and PR Personnel," or "Careers in Aerospace: Flying High, Flying Low?" The "Occupations" heading will often list bibliographic information on or cross-reference with special population groups, among other topics, such as "Blacks–Employment" or "Women–Employment." Articles indexed under these headings will lead to information addressing specific concerns, e.g., "Will Diversity = Opportunity + Advancement for Blacks?" or "The Ten Worst Careers for Women."

Finally, newspapers often have a jobs/careers section, usually as a Sunday supplement. Along with the classified job listings, there are often informative articles and regular columns.

Regular review of the above literature will not only allow a careers/jobs librarian current awareness, but also will extend to their helping career/job seekers find the information they need or could use. However, the knowledge base of a careers/jobs librarian should not stop at traditional sources. Useful materials extend well beyond the bounds of the "Vocational Guidance," "Occupations" or "Professions" subject categories.

NONTRADITIONAL SOURCES

There are "nontraditional" materials related to occupational literature in which careers/jobs coordinators should be aware of and ready to incorporate into their repertoire of sources used to help career/job seekers. Nontraditional material is most useful as a substitute when traditional career/job information is not readily available. This literature extends beyond the more obvious business-related directories or telephone books, and can involve a wide variety of sources too numerous to list here. The following discusses one idea for identifying an array of potentially useful literature to meet career/job needs. This approach is particularly significant in light of the development of online public access computers (OPACs), especially those having keyword access in title searches. The approach presumes that the keyword will be known and used in the search, and that the search does not result in an unmanageable number of items. A "nontraditional" approach to career/job literature will usually require more time to weed out irrelevant information. However, there are some gems that can be mined from the vast array of material available to search.

Many directories or guides have the potential to be useful in the careers/jobs arena. The best place to check for the existence of a directory is either in the *Directories in Print* (Detroit: Gale, 1980-. Biennial), or by typing the keywords "directory" and one or more other words in an online catalog. For instance, under "Foundation" there is the *Foundation Directory* (New York: Foundation Center, 1960-. Biennial) a directory of non-profit foundations or corporations involved with charitable giving, useful for individuals either interested in employment with a foundation or on a broader scale for those with backgrounds in public relations. Another example, in the health care field, is the American Hospital Association's *AHA Guide to the Health Care Field* (Chicago: AHA, 1972-. Annual). This reference lists things, such as hospices, medical and nursing licensure agencies, the headquarters of health care systems, including HMOs, and hospitals in the United States by state, including basic information about size, number of personnel and payroll. All of this information has great potential for the career/job seeker, for instance, having information on licensing agencies, or institutional, headquarters, or organizational addresses.

Many reference librarians are aware of sources, such as the *Gale Directory of Publications* (Detroit: Gale, 1987-. Annual). This publication lists information on newspapers, magazines, journals, radio and television stations, and cable systems. The entries are arranged by state, and subject indexes lead to specialized sections, such as black or Hispanic publications, trade publications, or radio stations and format. All of this information can help identify employer names and addresses, market sizes, and geographic boundaries, useful for individuals with backgrounds in journalism, broadcasting, or other occupations associated with these media.

The numerous "market place" titles, e.g., *The High Technology Market Place* (Middlebush, NJ: Princeton Hightech Group, 1990), can be used by anyone interested in the market place subject area listed in the title, including career/job seekers. Most are updated on a regular basis keeping the information current. For instance, the *Literary Market Place* (New York: Bowker, 1940-. Annual) lists most areas associated with the book publishing industry, such as book publishers, advertising agencies, prepress services, book distributors, employment agencies, and artists and art services. The *Direct Marketing Market Place* (Boca Raton, FL: Hilary House, 1980-. Annual) will give the career/job seeker with a business interest or background a list of service firms and suppliers, meetings and events, courses and seminars, direct marketing associations, clubs and organizations, as well as the direct marketers products and services.

Other specialized titles, such as those having the keywords "almanac" or "yearbook" in them often contain broad coverage of a subject area which can spill over into the careers/job area. For example, the *Computer Industry Almanac* by Karen Petska Juliussen and Egil Juliussen (New York: Brady, 1987-. Annual) is subtitled "the insider's guide to people, companies, products, and trends in the fascinating fast-paced computer industry." In addition, one chapter, entitled "Employment," leads to a variety of topics, for instance, "The Turbulent Job Market," or "Top 25 Electronics Employers." Another example, *Editor & Publisher International Yearbook* (New York: Editor and Publisher, 1921-. Annual) is advertised as having "more than 250,000 facts about newspapers" throughout the world.

Other examples of useful non-traditional occupational literature flourish. Literature searches can dwell in the area of "introduction to" type of titles found in numerous areas of specialization, and potentially useful to career planners when traditional career literature cannot be located. For instance, the career developer could make use of the following titles when related to their interests:

> Doheny, Margaret O'Bryan, *The Discipline of Nursing: an Introduction*, 2nd ed. (East Norwalk, CT: Appleton and Lange, 1987). The book has a chapter entitled, "Nursing as a Profession," useful for career planners;
> Baruth, Leroy G. *An Introduction to the Counseling Profession*, (Englewood Cliffs, NJ: Prentice Hall, 1987);
> Dalley, Tessa, ed. *Art as Therapy: An Introduction to the Use of Art as a Therapeutic Technique* (New York: Tavistock, 1984). This book not only introduces the many forms and uses of art as therapy, but also has a section on art therapy in practice.

NETWORKING

Serving as a strong complement to library resources are career/job resources in the community. In fact, addressing career/job needs is a community-wide effort, and libraries need to be part of this. Networking expands resources. Libraries need to work with professional community channels that provide for the individual in the career/job search process. Libraries are in the position of complementing the traditional career planning or job development department or agency in schools, colleges, and the community. There are many opportunities for networking, for instance:

- Libraries can expand on a job seekers natural network of friends and relatives by being networked with community resource persons, job clubs, or job development resource centers.
- Libraries can work with other job professionals to sponsor related workshops, job clubs, or support groups. A library is in a good position to do this considering its neutral orientation, community-based identity, and extended weekend and evening hours.

- A library can provide career/job service outreach to minorities by networking with local ethnic organizations.
- Libraries can network with school or college instructors or job search professionals who teach the career/job related classes or training programs. Library instruction could be worked into the course, and complement the syllabus by orienting the library instruction to meet certain goals or needs.
- Libraries can work with labor unions and pre-retirement programs as a means of marketing library services to adults and older adults in need of career/job assistance.
- Libraries can link with economic development agencies and departments of social service to provide a better understanding of each others services and reciprocal information and referral of services to those in need.

SUCCESSFUL SERVICES

The final part of this article will relate different scenarios successfully tried by libraries in providing career/job sources and services. The ideas in these capsulized versions are meant to provide possibilities for other libraries to consider trying. After all, these are needed sources and services. No library could go wrong in improving their services in this area, and most would not only help meet the needs of users, but also benefit in reputation and service delivery. The ideas and applications presented below should be combined with others presented throughout this entire issue of *The Reference Librarian*. The scenarios presented can be adapted, revised or expanded to meet unique situations, and many can move between the public, academic and special library domains.

- The Shields Library at the University of California-Davis, created a list of approximately 200 trade and professional journals, popular magazines, newspapers, and leaflets which consistently publish job openings in various disciplines (Opritsa, 1986).
- The InfoPLACE Program at the Cuyahoga County [Ohio] Public Library is an extensive career/job service facility that

hires both professional job counselors and librarians. Info-PLACE staff has a number of in-house guides and directories, including a regularly updated, heavily indexed "Education Directory." This directory indexes 6,000 non-credit courses offered in the area that are useful for those looking to upgrade their skills or education.

- San Diego State University library sponsored a workshop "Researching Employers" which complemented other workshops provided by the University's Center for Career Counseling and Placement (Rose, 1988).
- The Enoch Pratt Free Library, Baltimore, established a reciprocal referral career/job service by participation in Baltimore's Community Action Program. This involvement improved the library's image as a useable resource and allowed the librarian in the structure of other service providers (Gehlen, 1986).
- The University of Connecticut's Career Development Library staff developed a workbook to assist students in filling out the confusing Federal employment application form (SF-171). Second, the staff selected those job opportunities in government that were particularly appropriate for college graduates, rephrased the announcements, and published them in their regularly updated "Career Services Job Opportunities Bulletin." Finally, the staff indexed the internship files by paid and non-paid assignments, academic majors sought by employers, participating employers' names and locations, application deadlines, terms of the appointments, and stipend amounts, if any (Jacobson, 1991).
- Librarians at the Curricular-Career Information Center at Florida State University, Tallahassee, created with the assistance from career development professionals, a system for the management of career information. They combined traditional tools with tools specific to occupational information, and added a specialized subject index to nonoccupational career materials (Green, 1979).
- San Bernardino Public Library designed a project to integrate microcomputers into the library's public services area. One application was a career counseling service called "Micro-Quest." Combining disk and fiche, Micro-Quest provided up-

to-date career information for local citizens. On disk was a set of twenty one questions that identified an individual's capabilities, skills and other preferences. The program matched the users input to one of 450 occupations detailed on microfiche (Davis, Lambson and Whitney, 1987).

- The Texas State Technical Institute created a "Current Jobs Openings" section near the reference desk. There, current copies of publications such as *Career Opportunity Update*, *Federal Jobs Digest*, and *National Employment Opportunities Newsletter* were maintained.
- The COPES Center at the Flint [Michigan] Public Library traded a librarian position for a full time non-MLS career/job counselor. Among many activities, the Center works with ex-offenders referred to the Center by a local judge.

CONCLUSION

The library can no longer afford to be a marginal service in the delivery of career/job information. Its role is significant and can be made more significant given a commitment by the library's administration. The library's role is viable, and strongly complements the broader community picture of addressing the needs of career/job seekers. The role of libraries and its delivery of career/job services and sources is an extensive challenge. It is not enough for libraries to have just current occupational information available. Librarians need to be knowledgeable of current labor market direction and employment trends, establish clear access to career/job information, market the services available, and network with other career/job professionals in the community. By focusing on the needs of the community and deciding what career/job information can be realistically provided is one of the best moves a library can make.

REFERENCES

American Library Association (1989). Presidential Committee on Information Literacy. Final Report. January 1989. Chicago: American Library Association.
Davis, David M., Lambson, Norma, and Whitney, Stephen L. (1987). "Public Service Microcomputer Services in Public Libraries." *Library Journal*, 112 (18): 56, 58, 60+.

Durrance, Joan C. (1991). "Public Libraries and Career Changers: Insights from Kellogg-funded Sources." *Public Libraries*, 30 (2): 93-100.

Gehlen, Ann R. (1986). "Libraries and Employability," *Library Trends*, 35 (2): 303-309.

Green, Christine H. (1979). "Managing Career Information: A Librarian's Perspective." *Vocational Guidance Quarterly*, 28 (1): 83-91.

Jacobson, Bonnie and Palmer, Ray. (1991). "One Career Library Improves Its Image." *Journal of Career Planning and Employment*, 51 (3): 21-23.

Johnston, William B. (1987). *Workforce 2000: Work and Workers for the 21st Century*. Washington, DC: U. S. Government Printing Office for the Hudson Institute, Indianapolis, IN.

Opritsa, Popa, Hoffman, Irene and Firestein, Kenneth (1986). "Help Wanted: Job Listings in Journals–Tapping into the Library's Resources." *Research Strategies*, 4 (2): 68-74.

Rose, Robert F. (1988). "Conducting Research on Potential Employers: Report on a Cooperative Workshop." *RQ*, 27 (3): 404-409.

"The Shape of Things to Come" (1987). *Changing Times*, 41 (1): 28-47.

Silvestri, George, and Lukasiewicz, John (1989). "Projections of Occupational Employment, 1988-2000." *Monthly Labor Review*, 112 (11): 42-65.

Wegmann, Robert, Chapman, Robert, and Johnson, Miriam (1989). *Work in the New Economy: Careers and Job Seeking into the 21st Century*. Rev. ed. Indianapolis, IN: JIST Works).

LC Subject Headings
for Career Materials:
A Critique and Some Suggestions

William E. Studwell
David A. Hamilton

SUMMARY. The Library of Congress subject headings for careers and related topics are unsatisfactory for the needs of persons seeking such material. Some suggestions for improvement are offered.

INTRODUCTION

In the past decade or so, much literature has been devoted to the improvement of the Library of Congress subject headings, including suggestions for making better the headings for specific topics and disciplines. Among the special areas recently covered have been the disciplines of geology,[1] art,[2] and three particular aspects of literature, French fiction,[3] the form of names for literatures,[4] and women in literature.[5] One indicator of widespread interest in this type of small scale remedying is the three supportive letters, including one from Canada, received by the author of the article on art. Another indicator is the two different essays on LC headings for literature appearing in the same issue of one journal.[6]

In similar fashion, material on library services for careers and related topics have been receiving increased attention lately. The

---

William E. Studwell is Principal Cataloger and David A. Hamilton is General Reference Collection Development Coordinator, University Libraries, Northern Illinois University, DeKalb, IL 60115.

amount of material published on career planning and job hunting has steadily increased since the 1970s. Evidence of this lies in the abundance of books published by governmental agencies,[7] by private organizations based on government publications,[8] and by private organizations on their own.[9] There are a number of presses devoted primarily to career literature,[10] and a variety of popular titles are being updated on a regular basis.[11] There is even a bibliography issued bi-annually which tracks much of this growth and development.[12]

The number of pertinent articles also seems to be accelerating. In 1989, for example, there was a trilogy of articles linking libraries to career services. This included a report on career counseling in a public library,[13] a description of a job search library service in an academic library,[14] and an essay on career planning services and college libraries.[15] In addition, early in 1990, editors at *Choice* examined their policy toward career materials. Previously, career literature fell under *Choice's* general prohibition of how-to literature. Following further examination, certain career titles were seen as worthy of review. Now career literature is reviewed on a regular basis, so much so that recently a number of significant titles were cumulated into a review essay.[16]

It is apparent that both improvement of LC subject headings and interest in the careers field have been receiving more attention of late. In this study, the two trends come together. If careers is to be a significant facet of library service, then the LC headings which access such material should be made as understandable, appropriate, and as usable as possible.

THE PROBLEMS AND SOME SOLUTIONS

Any review of LC headings for a specific topic has to focus on the "red books",[17] LC's controlled vocabulary. It would be helpful to consult the "red books" while dealing with the complexities of the present article. Career related terms are found in various places in the "red books," but the primary or most important heading is "Vocational guidance." From this "grandparent" of career headings one can be referred to the related terms "Counseling," "Occupations," "Personnel service in education," "Professions," and "Vocational rehabilitation," and to allegedly subordinate terms such as "Career changes," "Career development," "Career plateaus," "Job hunting," "Occupations and race," "Vocational interests," and "Vocational qualifications." Immediately following "Vocational guidance" are some affiliated headings, "Vocational guidance for minorities," "Vocational guidance for the handicapped," and "Vocational guidance for women," plus some see references.

Believe it or not, the career field headings derivative of "Vocational guidance" are reasonably well done and effective. There are some minor problems, such as using the term "Job hunting" instead of "Job searching." LC uses "Job searching" as a reference to "Job hunting" and so despite the questionable choice of terminology, material is accessible. It is with the parent heading, however, where the main difficulties lie.

First, LC has put a lot of different eggs in the big basket they call "Vocational guidance." The complete listing of reference terms leading to "Vocational guidance" is:

> Business, Choice of
> Career counseling
> Career patterns
> Career planning
> Careers
> Choice of profession
> Guidance, Student
> Guidance, Vocational
> Occupation, Choice of
> Student guidance
> Vocation, Choice of
> Vocational opportunities

The terms stating or implying guidance or choice belong on this list, but the four terms with the word "career" or "careers" do not. LC has mixed together guidance on careers and choice of careers (or in other words, "which career") with the handling of careers (or in other words, "how"). "Career counseling" and "Career planning" are not really synonyms of "Vocational guidance," though they are related. To be counseled about careers and to plan a career are dissimilar enough from choosing a career to strongly justify separate headings for "Career counseling" and "Career planning." These two headings along with "Career changes," "Career development," "Career plateaus," and "Job hunting" which are associated with the handling of careers, should be made related terms. They all belong in the same list as "Occupations" and "Professions."

"Career patterns" and "Careers" are closely affiliated with "Occupations" and "Professions," and should not be references to "Vocational guidance." "Career patterns" and "Careers" currently also lead to the headings "Occupations" and "Professions" and this is entirely appropriate since all four terms, plus the other references "Jobs" and "Trades," all describe modes of work in a general way. However, "Career patterns" and "Careers" should be deleted as references to "Vocational guidance" because they do not directly equate to choice of career. Instead, "Careers, Choice of" and "Choice of careers" should be established as references to "Vocational guidance."

Second, except for the one "subordinate" heading "Job hunting," there is nothing under "Vocational guidance" to lead the user to related terms beginning with "Job" ("Job offers," "Job postings," "Job vacancies," etc.). At the least, LC could make a "see also" ("SA") note under "Vocational guidance" leading to headings beginning with "Job," and should do the same under "Occupations" and "Professions."

Third, the subdivision "Vocational guidance," which is used after "professions, fields of knowledge, industries, names of corporate bodies, and individual military services," is a problem. When material is clearly intended to be an aid in selecting a career, the subdivision works out well and does not confuse the user. However, in practice material on preparing for a specific occupation and material on the operational or psychological characteristics of a specific occupation are often given the subdivision "Vocational guidance." If, for example, a book is on education for a nursing career, the heading should be "Nursing–Study and teaching." The choice of career and preparation for a career are related, they are different. And if, for example, a book is about the everyday duties of nurses, or the psychological ramifications of nursing, the headings "Nursing" and "Nursing–Psychological aspects" would be appropriate. In neither of these examples would "Vocational guidance" be a suitable heading, since the purposes are not to help choose an occupation but to describe an occupation for other reasons.

Therefore, LC should make a note under "Vocational guidance" outlining the alternative of using the subdivision "Study and teaching" for works on education for an occupation, and a note outlining the alternative of using the name of the occupation with other subdivisions such as "Psychological aspects" or "Social aspects," or the name without subdivision, when other characteristics of the occupation are being treated. All facets of an occupation cannot be lumped under the subdivision "Vocational guidance." Subject headings should clearly differentiate between the aspects, and such differentiation should also be clearly documented.

Burying one's head in the sand, and jumbling up or glossing over related but discrete topics helps nobody. If a work is on more than one aspect of an occupation, more than one heading should be applied. For instance, a book on choosing nursing as a career and also substantially on education for such a career should be serviced by a pair of headings, "Nursing–Vocational guidance" and "Nursing–Study and teaching." The heading "Nursing" by itself would be too vague, especially since only two aspects of nursing are covered, and "Nursing–Vocational guidance" by itself would be incomplete and too narrow.

Another problem with the subdivision "Vocational guidance" is its structure ("[Occupation]–Vocational guidance"). Persons looking for vocational guidance materials on a variety of occupations have to search under each individual occupation, since "Vocational guidance" is not the initial element. This is not a concern in very sophisticated online catalogs which have the capability to search every subject element in any order.[18] But it creates difficulties in any system of lesser characteristics. However, if the structure of "Vocational guidance–[Occupation]," an equally troublesome dilemma is created. If such a move were made, both a theoretical problem and a practical problem would appear. On a theoretical basis, the heading for the occupation would be a subdivision and not the initial element, while in other situations the occupation would be the initial element. On a practical basis, the searcher might not be aware that the occupation could be used as a subdivision under "Vocational guidance."

Under current LC subject heading structure, there is no good answer to this dilemma. The only type of punctuation LC presently allows between headings is the dash, which tends to suggest subordination. However, "Vocational guidance" is not a subordinate concept but instead a more or less equal term to the specific occupation. That's where the basic trouble lies. If LC developed a relational structure using a slash between two basically equal topics, the result "[Occupation]/Vocational guidance" would be theoretically sound.[19] It still could not be retrieved any easier until a sophisticated online catalog like the one mentioned above was available. Although such online catalogs could also access "[Occupation]–Vocational guidance" with equal ease, the advantages of logical superiority would be lost with the dash structure.

CONCLUSION

With the large amount of career materials in libraries and an apparent increase in servicing these, enhanced subject access to career materials is vital. By clearly differentiating between related terms in the field, and by documenting application policies in the "red books" so that all can see them, LC could improve subject retrieval relating to career materials. Career choices and career handling are difficult enough without also having to grope around or be confused in the library environment.

REFERENCES

1. Studwell, William E. and Larsgaard, Mary L., "Geologic Subject Headings: A Macro View and a Micro View," *Western Association of Map Libraries Information Bulletin*, 21, no. 1 (November 1989): 56-59.

2. Studwell, William E., "Subject Suggestions 5: Some Concerns Relating to Art," *Cataloging & Classification Quarterly*, 10, 3 (1990): 91-95.

3. DeHart, Florence E. and Matthews, Karen, "French Fiction: LCSH Applications," *Cataloging & Classification Quarterly*, 9, 2 (1988): 3-24.

4. Studwell, William E., "Subject Suggestions 3: The Form of Name for Literatures," *Cataloging & Classification Quarterly*, 9, 2 (1988): 93-100.

5. Mowery, Robert L., "Women in Literature: A Study of Library of Congress Subject Cataloging," *Cataloging & Classification Quarterly*, 9, 4 (1989): 89-99.

6. See notes 3 and 4.

7. Particularly significant are the regularly issued publications of the U. S. Department of Labor, such as, *Occupational Outlook Handbook, 1990-91* (biannual), *Dictionary of Occupational Titles*, 4th ed. rev., 1991, and *Handbook of Labor Statistics* (annual).

8. For example, *Exploring Careers*, rev. ed. Indianapolis, IN: JIST Works, 1990.

9. For example, *Professional Careers Sourcebook: An Information Guide for Career Planning*. Detroit, MI: Gale Research, 1990.

10. For example, The Career Press, Inc., Hawthorne, NJ: Bob Adams, Inc., Holbrook, MA: and VGM Career Horizons, Lincolnwood, IL.

11. For example, Bolles, Richard Nelson, *What Color Is Your Parachute?* Berkeley, CA: Ten Speed Press, annual; *Career Information Center*, 4th ed., 13 vols. Encino, CA: Glencoe/Macmillan, 1990; and *Encyclopedia of Careers and Vocational Guidance*, 8th ed. Chicago, IL: Ferguson, 1990.

12. *Where to Start Career Planning: Essential Resource Guide for Career Planning and Job Hunting*, 7th ed., 1990-91 Ithaca, NY: Cornell University, 1990."

13. Rome, Linda, "InfoPLACE: Career Counseling at Cuyahoga County," *Wilson Library Bulletin*, 63 (January 1989): 74-75.

14. Windsor, Laura, "The Academic Reference Librarian: Serving Graduates in Their Job Search," *College and Research Library News*, 50 (July/August 1989): 577-579.

15. Anderson, Byron, "Working with Your College Library," *Journal of Career Planning and Employment*, 44, 4 (Summer 1989): 46-49.

16. Anderson, Byron with the assistance of Dorothy E. Jones, "Career Literature: A Survey of Recent Works," *Choice*, 28, 2 (October 1990): 267.

17. *Library of Congress Subject Headings*, 13th ed. Washington, DC: Library of Congress, 1990.

18. For more on online catalogs with such capabilities, see William E. Studwell, "Retrieving LC Subject Headings: Long Chains Versus an Increased Number of Headings." *Technicalities*, 9, 9 (September 1989): 8-9.

19. For more on the relational slash, see William E. Studwell, *Library of Congress Subject Headings: Philosophy, Practice, and Prospects*. New York: The Haworth Press, Inc, 1990, pp. 33-36.

II. CAREER PLANNING AND JOB SEARCHING: LIBRARY SERVICES AND COOPERATIVE PROGRAMS

The Training of Librarians to Work with the Adult Unemployed: The Pennsylvania Model

Stephen M. Mallinger

SUMMARY. In 1987, the W. K. Kellogg Foundation gave a grant to the State Library of Pennsylvania to establish a program to work with unemployed adults. The grant established six sites called WORK-PLACE. A key factor in establishing a WORKPLACE site was the inclusion of a trained librarian on the staff who served in the role as a professional counselor. The chapter discusses the training that was provided and the lessons learned. Today, there are seventy five Pennsylvania libraries offering WORKPLACE service. The most effective "resource" at these sites as related by WORKPLACE users has been the librarian.

Stephen M. Mallinger is the Library Development Advisor at the State Library of Pennsylvania, Harrisburg, PA 17105.

INTRODUCTION

In 1987, the W. K. Kellogg Foundation awarded a grant of $673, 000 to the State Library of Pennsylvania to establish the Education Information Center (EIC) program in the Commonwealth. The Education Information Center concept was premised on the belief that adults were life long learners in need of information to assist in that pursuit. An information center was needed to gather, organize and disseminate this information. The learner or client would then be assisted by a center staff member to help in the decision making about future learning paths. In 1978, the Kellogg Foundation funded the Westchester Education Brokering Service (WEBS) at the Westchester Public Library. This library project narrowed the learning needs of the clients to economic concerns, adapted the WEBS project and established WORKPLACE, the sites of career information service in Pennsylvania public libraries. Stephen Mallinger was assigned to be the WORKPLACE project director.

THE EIC PROJECT

Pennsylvania's EIC project was similar to WEBS in that the clients would be the adult in career transition. Dislocated workers, single mothers, hard core unemployed and youth at risk were the target groups. But the Pennsylvania project differed in three important ways: the State Library would coordinate a unified project in six pilot sites, the WORKPLACE sites would all incorporate computer decision making software, and librarians would be the service providers. The last characteristic is the most important. In WEBS, the career information service sites were staffed by professional career counselors. Often the librarians were neutral to the service. The counselors learned about libraries by observing and interacting with other library staff. The State Library realized that if the service were to succeed and continue, the libraries must incorporate WORKPLACE into their standard public library reference service. These career information stations must not be a library housed but a library based service.

The State Library selected the six sites through a careful process. Only the twenty six district library centers were eligible. The sites were required to permit a full time professional librarian on their staff to manage the project, attend the intensive planned training, and coordinate the site's activities with the other project pilot sites. This requirement to include the active and long term participation of a professional librarian was the main reason that most libraries refused to enter the project even though there was ample funding. The State Library did not back down from this requirement. From the inception of the WORKPLACE project, the State Library realized that the key factor was the active support of professional staff. WORKPLACE had to be more than merely purchasing equipment and other resources. The project applications encouraged the libraries to select professional librarians with both "people skills and an interest in computer technology."

THE TRAINING PLAN

After six pilot sites were selected and the project librarians identified, the State Library immediately instituted the WORKPLACE training program. The training plan was developed to include the following:

1. Training sessions were to be held every two months at different locations around the state.
2. All training was to concentrate around the three basic WORKPLACE concepts of understanding the information needs of the adult in career transition, computer guidance, and linkage with the community.
3. Project librarians were encouraged to supplement their State Library workshops with training sponsored by the Kellogg Foundation or any other relevant program approved by the State Library.
4. All training received by the project librarians was to be disseminated to the other staff members of the pilot libraries.

5. All training would be based on Pennsylvania library conditions and needs. No previous EIC program would be copied.

The group was cohesive and quickly formed a esprit de corps.
Four were reference librarians, one was a former children's librarian, and one was a branch library manager. All had their MLS degree and were highly committed to strong professional service.
Only one librarian had previously worked with career information
services. All had been "volunteered," and were highly suspicious
of the project. None had ever received any kind of previous training
to serve the unemployed either in library school or in their own
libraries.

The State Library staff had already received an orientation to
EIC's, but every effort was made to develop the WORKPLACE
training as the project developed. In other words, as we received
information from the sites we would determine the training needs
of the staff. This often created conflicts with established EIC models in other states which had been staffed by non-librarians. But the
State Library was determined to develop a truly viable Pennsylvania
library EIC model.

The Kellogg Foundation had contracted with a training team to
both introduce the initial training models and service as consultants
to the four state libraries participating in the project. The team
included both educators from university guidance education facul-
ties and the former director of the WEBS project. In late 1987, the
four state libraries sent their project staff to Kansas City for the
initial training. Only Pennsylvania's team were all professional
librarians. Other states included academics, professional guidance
counselors and adult educators. This Kansas training introduced
various theories of learning as well as techniques on working with
the unemployed. Some of the other states' teams were impatient
with these models of understanding the project and preferred to use
their own counseling background to develop their programs. A clear
division arose whether selecting librarians to work with unemployed
adults was feasible. Some counselors felt that librarians were too
mechanistic to deal with the adult in transition. One professor of
education remarked that librarians should ". . . go back to shelving

the books.'' The Pennsylvania librarians clearly felt that the trainers had relevancy, but little understanding of libraries or librarians.

After returning from Kansas, the State Library began their training. Every two months, the three day training was held. Attendance was required, and the librarians were encouraged to socialize together. Evening sessions were avoided to encourage a more positive attitude to the training. This was very effective. While the training was generally in Pennsylvania libraries, the entire group was taken to New Orleans and Dallas for meetings of the ALA EIC project libraries. Training was held at the annual meeting of the Pennsylvania Library Association and the Public Library Association which met in Pennsylvania one year. At the last two meetings, the WORKPLACE libraries manned the State Library exhibit booth to gain experience in presenting the project to the public. Non-State Library training was at adult literacy conferences, workshops on computers, and government job training programs. Every State Library training included the same three concepts mentioned above: understand the client, using computers to develop client service, and community linkage. At the workshop on working with the local job service, the librarians were required to bring along the manager of their area state job service office. The State Library paid the expenses for these other attendees.

The State Library attempted to use faculty from the state's three accredited library schools to assist in the training. Unfortunately, this did not occur. There was little interest, and most library educators felt ill prepared in this area. The instructors came from three fields: state agencies that worked with adult unemployment and retraining, career counselors that were experienced with computer assisted decision making, and professionals who worked with special needs clients. Dr. Nancy Schlossberg's theory of the ''Career Decision Making Wheel'' was accepted and incorporated into all aspects of the WORKPLACE training. This model divides career information into four parts of a wheel: knowing yourself, knowing the world of work, making decisions, and taking action. Librarians were encouraged to apply resources based on the various sections or stages on the wheel. For example, when the client needed to understand their abilities in relation to the world of work, the librarian would prescribe the client to use the self assessment module of the DISCOVER software program. Since every WORKPLACE site received the same start up computer system, career guidance software, and video job search tutorial, it was easy to provide uniform training. At one training, the librarians received presentations from the three major career guidance software developers. No technology was ever presented without "hands on" opportunities, and every librarian had their own terminal to use.

The WORKPLACE librarians attended ten training sessions over a two year period. At the end of the grant project, the training was discontinued. All WORKPLACE sites have continued. Of the original six librarians, five are still active in their programs. The other librarian has left the state. The State Library later expanded the program with Job Training Partnership Act (JTPA) funds. There are now seventy five libraries (including fifteen prison libraries) presently offering WORKPLACE service in the state. A video explaining the program was produced, and a training manual published. Training is still provided, but the training time is now only two days. Over 100 librarians are now trained. To date, no library school has yet introduced the training in their regular coursework. The training is still supervised by Stephen Mallinger.

LESSONS LEARNED

During the training, the State Library has learned important facts on how to train librarians to work with the unemployed. These include:

1. Librarians do not accept the term "career counselors" or "career advisors." Counseling has connotations of therapy, illness and mental health. All of these make the librarians highly uncomfortable. The term preferred is "effective reference librarian."

2. Librarians are impatient with theory. They prefer to learn experientially, and are anxious to see and learn how to use re-

sources. They do, however, need a basic model as a framework for operating their client service.

3. Librarians learn best from other librarians who are doing similar things. This feeling was best expressed by one project participant as ". . . don't tell me anything until you have actually been down here on the floor or behind the reference desk and know what it is like; then I will believe you." If non-librarians are the trainers, their own attitudes to the library profession and knowledge about libraries should be reviewed.

4. The leading concern about working with unemployed people in a library is the lack of time. Traditional practice has taught that reference interviews are quick, one time experiences. The WORKPLACE training encourages the librarians to schedule appointments, train other staff and community agency people to assist in the service.

5. Librarians fully accept computers for assistance to patrons or clients. But unless the librarians are fully trained, have technical support which they can call upon at will, and have reliable equipment, they will not disseminate computer use to the public.

6. Librarians must be taught their authentic and legitimate role. It is not to find a job for every unemployed library patron, nor help these clients "find themselves," nor type resumes for patrons. THE ROLE IS TO PROVIDE INFORMATION TO HELP ADULTS IN CAREER TRANSITION MAKE DECISIONS ABOUT THEIR ECONOMIC FUTURE. As a corollary to this role, WORKPLACE librarians are taught to:

     a. listen to the client's problem
     b. diagnose the client's information needs
     c. prescribe the resources to use
     d. facilitate use of the resources.

7. Librarians must always be permitted the latitude to design the career information service model on their own needs, limitations, and setting. This must be clearly understood and repeated in the training. They must understand that they have

the power to make the service succeed or fail depending on their own emotional attitude to this.

8. In any effective training, the librarians should be introduced to local, state and national community resource people. Names, addresses, and phone numbers must be provided. Names and locations of similar projects should be included and networking should begin during the training.

9. Librarians must understand that career information service is primarily an adult directed service, not the traditional "career corner" where college catalogs are stacked. They must be taught that unemployed adults have other information problems; literacy, stress, addiction, financial crises, etc., that must be addressed.

10. Lastly, training must include techniques to promote the service.

In the last four years, over 90,000 people have used WORK-PLACE sites in Pennsylvania's public and prison libraries. The State Library with the assistance of the Kellogg Foundation evaluated the effect of the project. It was interesting that in all six sites, the most effective "resource" cited by WORKPLACE users was the librarian. It was also observed that the new sites with the strongest commitment to the WORKPLACE were the sites with librarians who received training. The implication that similar training for service to other special client groups should be replicated is very strong.

TRAINING SCHEDULE AGENDA

"WORKPLACE LIBRARY SERVICE TO DISLOCATED WORKERS"

(First day)

9:00 a.m.	Coffee and pastry
9:15	Introduction to the WORKPLACE Project
10:00	The Information Needs of Dislocated Workers
11:00	WORKPLACE Site Resources

12:00	Lunch
1:00	Computer Career Guidance
2:00	PERFECT RESUME
4:00	Working with Clients
5:00	Adjourn

(Second day)

9:00 a.m.	DISCOVER Software
12:00	Lunch
1:00	PA CAREERS Software
3:00	PHEAA Software–KEYS, PAIS, RESUME 1
5:00	Adjourn

(Third day)

9:00 a.m.	Video Job Search Workshops
11:00	Managing a WORKPLACE Site
12:00	Lunch
1:00	Linking with JTPA
3:00	The Training is Adjourned

A Survey of Cooperative Activities Between Career Planning Departments and Academic Libraries

Charlene Abel

SUMMARY. Cooperative efforts between academic libraries and career planning departments are examined. Such efforts are deemed to be rather lackluster. The Career Information Center at DePaul University is discussed as a positive example of the benefits to be derived through information and resource sharing between two such departments.

THE SURVEY

The author set out to examine activities of career planning departments and academic libraries in the areas of career development and job searching. The specific aim was to look for areas of cooperation between the two agencies within an academic setting.

A literature search was done and questionnaires were sent to fifty colleges and universities, most of them in the midwest. A mix of libraries and career planning offices was included in the mailing of the questionnaires. A request for information was also sent to two electronic discussion lists.

Questions focused on the topics of collection location, access through computer systems or bibliographies, present or past programs, and plans for future activities.

Charlene Abel is Reference Librarian, DePaul University Loop Campus Library, 25 East Jackson, Chicago, IL 60604.

Key Questions Asked

(CP = Career Planning; LIB = Library)

	CP		LIB	
	yes	no	yes	no
Do you maintain a career collection separate from the main library collection?	16	1	9	17
Is there an individual responsible for selecting career materials?	13	2	10	9
Do you compile lists of career sources in your collection?	9	7	10	17
Is there computerized access to your collection?	4	13	not asked	
Does the library receive notice of recruiters coming on campus?	6	11	9	14
Do you present seminars on career related issues?	16	1	8	17
Are the seminars done cooperatively with CP/LIB?	4	12	6	4
Has the library done seminars for placement staff?	5	12	2	23
Has CP publicized library services?	9	8	3	20
Has CP funded the library in any way?	0	15	1	24

Cooperative Projects

Career planning departments were asked to describe cooperative projects they had participated in with their institutions' libraries. This is a selection of these comments:

"We provide activity/program information to library for 'News' database"

"We keep a notebook of library information on file in resource center"

"We have several job search guidebooks on reserve at the library"

"I prefer to keep the bulk of our career search related materials in the library. A student will not always have a placement office near, if at all, but will usually have access to a library"

"We refer students to the reference desk if no material available"

"The Library maintains a few career resources such as S&P, Moody's, listing of associations, etc. The career center acquires and maintains other reference material. In isolated cases, items are a joint purchase (video & film)"

"The career library receives some of the career-related depository materials from the government publications department. New reference librarians get a tour of the career library. Career brochures are kept in main library. The campus libraries' holdings are on the main frame and accessible from various terminals in the career center and elsewhere"

"Updating and expanding our (and the library's) corporate files. Centralized and organized the access to graduate catalog information. Gained access to their career holdings through our campus computer system"

Libraries were asked to describe projects done in cooperation with their institutions' career planning departments. Below are some of their comments:

"Assisted in the compilation of lists of periodicals which carry job postings and are held by MSU libraries. (Lists tailored for engineering, arts & humanities, business, etc.)"

"Contact 12 placement offices on IU-Bloomington campus at least twice a year to remind them of library resources"

"Exchange resource lists (in computer database form). Post Career Development notices in Career Reference area"

"None for us. All-in-all this area is a low key, low priority for us"

"How depressing my answers are! You have gotten me to think about our lack of cooperation with the placement office–maybe we can do something in the future"

"Offer annual sessions on library resources/information sources"

"Our placement office runs its own small resource center. We do make sure all new reference librarians tour their center and have a good grasp of what's available there. Our biggest headache is the unexpected presence of campus interviewers for "teeny" companies which we can find no published information; I really don't care to be notified–I'd like them to make clear to students who sign up–what exists and where to find it"

"All we've done so far are the bibliographies and job workshops with specific professors (Marketing, etc.)"

"We did online company searches in the past for companies coming to recruit but it became too expensive for us as the career office paid nothing and wanted us to search a large number (50+) effectively bypassing information sources already in library (paper and indexes)"

"We have offered "Careers in Librarianship" sessions under (Placement Office) sponsorship several times"

"We share pamphlets and publications. I send them extras and they send me theirs. I give a lecture in the placement office's class that has to do with careers"

"Occasionally send government document career opportunities as received in our capacity as government document library"

"All we are doing at present is compiling a list of job ads in the science journals. Prospective employees would be able to look up a job title or area to find journals (in our library) containing ads in that field"

Future Projects

Career planning departments were asked what projects were planned for the future:

"Teaming for presentations"

"Working on master list of our titles to be put in library system. We often use each other for referral purposes with students"

"Have not discussed this yet, but plan to talk to reference librarian re: creating a list of career publications and/or system for improving access to career materials"

Libraries were asked what projects were being planned in conjunction with career planning departments for the future:

"Planning to expand availability of career information sources for short term loan"

"Have worked with Office of Financial Aid which is providing a scholarship search service and will be making students aware of this service"

"Continue to increase the amount of information available on careers in the 11 halls of residence libraries–thereby decentralizing access to this type of information"

"None"

"We plan to work together on seminar for placement office staff utilizing library resources as well as provide career seminars for students with placement rather than only through specific courses"

"I plan to (a) prepare pathfinder, (b) new books list (c) turn in article to the Placement Office Newsletter"

"None, but your questionnaire has really made me think"

"I would like to work with the career services center and a librarian in the humanities/social science library to be involved in career seminar–present job and career sources available in the library"

SURVEY SUMMARY

In essence, there does not seem to be a great deal of sharing of information between career planning departments and libraries. While excellent programs and supports are available at many institutions such as Harvard's Baker Library and the University of Illinois for example, institutions with fewer resources and need for resource sharing have not taken the cue from the larger, better funded institutions. Efforts to provide access to each other's resources seem rather lackluster.

Only four career planning respondents said that their collections were in the library's online catalog. One respondent reported that the library and career planning departments periodically exchange collection holdings on floppy disks.

One activity apparently gaining interest was reported in the literature (Popa et al., 1986) and by two respondents. It entails the compilation of library sources carrying job listings, a type of service that should be appreciated by today's busy students since one of the most recent reference sources published for this purpose (Feingold & Hansard-Winkler, 1989) is cumbersome to use.

A number of respondents provided samples of their career bibliographies. Out of a total forty eight responses, not quite half provide bibliographies for their clientele. The publications received were all well organized and seemingly heavily used at their respective campuses. One interesting fact is that rarely did one department refer to another's resources or services in more than a passing way. The American University sent a bibliography which included information on resources in both the library and the career center.

Few cooperative seminars were reported, though these would seem natural areas for academic librarians to perform their teaching function. Windsor (1989) reports a library's presentation for students in the computer field. Rose (1988) reported a cooperative workshop on conducting research on potential employers. Two library respondents reported library participation in credit courses offered at their institutions. Gliken (1986) reports on several lectures given by a foreign languages librarian concerning foreign languages and careers. The article stated that one objective of the lectures was to "bring the attention of the rest of the campus to the usefulness of the library in the job search" (p. 2).

A respondent reported the library's role in providing career information was in searching, often online, with most information provided on demand. Gathering information on companies that will be interviewing on campus does not seem to be a common practice.

As Windsor (1989) says in her discussion of a job searching seminar for computer science students, "most of us will show them adequate reference sources but our role in a students quest for employment is many times seen as minimal . . ." (p. 577).

ONE UNIVERSITY'S EXAMPLE

Even at the risk of offering a "how we do it good" lecture, it seems appropriate to present a brief overview of one career collection within a library setting. This program has been deemed a success by all involved–Career Planning and Placement, library staff, and students.

The Career Information Center (CIC) at DePaul University's Loop Campus Library is the result of a proposal presented by the College of Commerce Dean's Student Advisory Council Career Planning Information Center Committee.

A finding of this committee was that "students are both unaware and reluctant to utilize the somewhat scattered resource base found here." This report stated that: "The goal of a Career Planning Information Center at De Paul should seek to overcome (1) the lack of a central location for resource material; (2) inadequate student/resource ratio; (3) inability of young students to feel comfortable and knowledgeable about the center through proper promotion and orientation; (4) need for a resource staff person to coordinate center and update resource base" (Dean's Student Advisory Council, 1987).

By the Fall of 1987, the joint efforts of De Paul's College of Commerce, Career Planning and Placement (CP&P), and the library resulted in the Center being opened in a 280 square foot space near the Loop Campus Library entrance and adjacent to the reference desk.

A reference librarian was appointed career bibliographer with a budget, and mandated to purchase across subject lines. Sources such as company brochures and recruiting manuals were sent from the Career Planning and Placement Office to the library. Books on resume writing were pulled from the reference stacks and placed together in the Center. Books and serials purchased with the new budget were shelved in the Center to form a core reference collection. A computer workstation was installed for dial-in access to DISCOVER, a career guidance program.

A list of materials ordered was created using Procite software. The index feature allows specialized subject lists to be generated as needed. These lists are housed at both campus libraries and at both Career Planning and Placement offices. With a good reference core established, more circulating materials are being added for the increased convenience of students. The Library maintains the collection of company brochures and recruiting manuals. CP&P staff suggests materials for purchase and has donated some review copies of books.

So well received was the Career Information Center at the Loop Campus Library that the library administration and collection development committee deemed it of great enough importance to offer the same library services at the Lincoln Park Campus. (The Loop Campus Library collection primarily supports the curriculum of the College of Commerce while the Lincoln Park Campus supports the College of Liberal Arts and Sciences, the Theater School, and the Music School.) In fiscal year 1989/90, the career materials budget was doubled to strengthen the career collection at the north campus. In Spring 1992 the Lincoln Park Library will move into a large new facility where a Career Information Center is to be located just off the entrance lobby. Career Planning and Placement is working with the library director to acquire corporate funding for the Center's furnishings in the new library.

At times, DePaul's CP&P has supplemented the library's career budget by contributing dollars for some large ticket items. A film collection was purchased, as was a subscription to Peterson's *Gradline* CD-ROM. In the past CP&P provided the Discover program, and purchased Dun & Bradstreet credit report units for information on private companies.

Using Procite software, mini-bibliographies on various topics are generated for publication in CP&P's *Job Opportunities Bulletin*. CP&P prints information about the library in its quarterly newsletter, its biweekly recruiting schedule, and in the previously mentioned *J.O.B.*

The library examines CP&P's recruiting schedules and does basic research on the companies. This information is maintained in chart form using PC File+. Librarians at the reference desk appreciate having some of the basic sources searched in advance. The library is considering the possibility of mounting the week's recruiting schedule on the university's Vax main frame.

Displays of career materials are regularly featured. A future project is the posting of library displays within the CP&P offices of the recruiting list research and book jackets.

The Library has given tours to CP&P staff. The career bibliographer and liaison have been asked to present a seminar on library resources for CP&P staff during the summer of 1991. It is hoped that this seminar also can be presented on a regular basis as part of CP&P's student programs.

The two departments have outlined a career brochure which would describe services offered by CP&P and other sources in the libraries. Staff members from both areas are to contribute. At present the library maintains a subject list of all books cataloged or ordered for the career collection, and distributes it to both library reference departments and CP&P offices.

Since the opening of the Loop Campus CIC in 1987, a smooth working relationship has developed between the library and CP&P. Services have benefited both departments and most of all the student body. There has been no usurpation of responsibilities, dollars, or staffing. ''Naturally, no one would suppose that librarians should or could usurp a counselor's authority or position. But working together, these professionals are able to open previously unavailable or unknown alternatives to students seeking career information'' (Lary, 1985, p. 505).

CONCLUSION

It can be strongly stated that more communication is needed between libraries and career planning departments. While departments' situations vary widely due to institution size, finances, campus locations, and other factors, opportunities exist for coordination that results in better access to resources and services.

Consider this statement coming from a career planning department, "We send students to the reference desk if we don't have anything" and the statement ". . . or if you are in a hurry, ask a reference librarian" from a recently published book (Steele & Morgan, 1991). Both bespeak rather cavalier attitudes toward both libraries and career information sources. Hopefully the attitude would be more like Anderson's who stated, "Cooperation between college librarians and career development professionals can strengthen available career information and enhance its access, make career development professionals better counselors, and extend relevant library services to their clientele" (Anderson, 1989, p. 46).

The examples presented of activities at DePaul and other colleges and universities reveal the benefits of cooperative programs that can be realized through reasonable amounts of time, resources, and effort. Comments from career planning departments and libraries that have worked together reflect the usefulness of integrating the library into job search and career decision activities on campus.

REFERENCES

Anderson, B. (1989). Working with your college library. *Journal of Career Planning and Employment*, 49 (4): 46-49.

Dean's Student Advisory Council. Career Planning Information Center Committee (1987). Proposal for establishment of a center. Unpublished report, DePaul University, College of Commerce, Chicago.

Feingold, S.N., & Hansard-Winkler, G.A. (1989). *Where the jobs are: A comprehensive directory of 1200 journals listing career opportunities*. Garrett Park, MD: Garrett Park Press.

Gliken, R. (1986). *Career education: Foreign languages and the librarian*. (Viewpoints) (ERIC Document Reproduction Service no. ED 273 130)

Lary, M.S. (1985). Career resources centers. *Library Trends*, 33 (4): 501-512.

Popa, O., Hoffman, I., & Firestein, K. (1986). Help wanted: job listings in journals–tapping into the library's resources. *Research Strategies*, 4 (2): 68-74.

Rose, R.F. (1988). Conducting research on potential employers: Report on a cooperative workshop. *RQ*, 27 (3): 404-409.

Steele, J.E., & Morgan, M.S. (1991). *Career planning and development for college students and recent graduates*. Lincolnwood, IL: VGM Career Horizons.

Windsor, L. (1989, July). The academic reference librarian: Serving graduates in their job search. *College & Research Libraries News*, 7, 577-579.

The Career Center Library:
A Special Library
in an Academic Setting

Elizabeth A. Lorenzen
Sarah Jane Batt

SUMMARY. Every college or university has resources on career development available somewhere, and frequently in more than one place. Too often, however, students do not know where those resources are located. Even more often, once they have found the resources, students do not know how to use them effectively in either career planning or the job search. The Career Center Library (CCL) at Indiana State University has proved to be an innovative solution to this problem. Located in the Career Center, one block from the University's main library, the CCL is considered to be a satellite of the ISU Libraries system. The Career Center librarian is a member of the library faculty who has been funded by and assigned to the Student Services Division of the University to provide both reference and collection development services for the Division. Support is available through ISU Libraries and therefore, access to information resources is enhanced. CCL resources are easily accessible through ISU Libraries' online catalog. This chapter will discuss the development of the Career Center Library at ISU and will illustrate special developments which arose during the process of its organization.

Elizabeth A. Lorenzen is the Career Center Librarian at the Career Center, Student Services Building, Indiana State University, Terre Haute, IN 47809. Sarah Jane Batt, formerly Career Center Librarian at Indiana State University, is a reference librarian at the Indianapolis-Marion County Public Library, 40 East St. Clair Street, Indianapolis, IN 46221.

61

INTRODUCTION

Indiana State University (ISU), located in west central Indiana, draws students from various backgrounds to pursue a wide variety of liberal arts, business, education, science and technological studies, with a few select programs culminating in a Ph.D. degree. Approximately 12,000 students come from all over the United States and many foreign countries. ISU Libraries, with holdings of approximately 1.8 million, has a main library and three additional special libraries, one being the Career Center Library. It employs twenty-nine librarians and forty-eight support staff, and was the first academic library in the State of Indiana to fully automate, using NOTIS as an integrated online library system.

As is common on most campuses, the diverse student population coming to ISU's campus arrives with varying degrees of preparedness for a college education, and, naturally, with diverse career goals. ISU's comprehensive Career Center provides a range of career services to accommodate not just the diverse career goals, but also the varying levels of career development of ISU's students. New students of both traditional and non-traditional age may all need help assessing strengths, identifying interests and selecting a major, but they need that help to take different forms. Students ready to graduate may arrive seeking help with their resume, yet may not have formulated a career objective. Career Center counselors in Career Planning, Professional Practice Programs, and Placement Services regularly refer students to each other in order to best meet the individual students' needs. The Career Center librarian is involved in the Center's operations and actively serves the information needs of the Career Center staff.

THE ENVIRONMENT

When academic librarians and career counselors are engaged in providing information to students on career development in an academic setting, several problems may arise. Most of those problems can be attributed to a lack of communication. Although students interact with career counselors on a regular basis, they may not be aware of the resources available to them unless the counselor is knowledgeable about such resources and their potential benefits. Career counselors may be aware of some of the types of resources available, but without a background in librarianship, they may not be able to use resources effectively, organize them efficiently, make them easily accessible to themselves, or make them known beyond the confines of their own organization.

Students going through the process of career development are usually in a time of great indecision. Even when they have a general career direction, they rarely know what resources they want or need in order to accomplish their goals. In providing either reference service or career counseling to these students, it is important not only to give them what they need, but to understand and help them understand that they may not know what they need and that there is nothing wrong with that admission.[1] Librarians, while skilled reference interviewers, may be unable to fully meet the needs of these students. Academic librarians also may have difficulty selecting materials to support the university's career services program because they may not fully understand the services it provides. Career professionals are a good resource for defining needs and trends, and they know how to locate ephemeral employer information and job vacancy lists. These types of resources are difficult to locate if one is not actively working in the field of career development.

In maintaining a collection which supports career development activities, currency and ease of access must be of the utmost importance. When the resources and services are centralized and managed by one person, a librarian, communication about resources and services is enhanced and, at the same time, overlap, duplication, and gaps are more easily avoided. The organization and management of the collection needs to be a centralized process in order to ensure consistency and effectiveness.[2] Librarians can help both counselor and student find appropriate career resources, no matter how nontraditional the service or format might be. More frequent interaction between counselors and librarians will provide both with a better understanding of their respective services. A better understanding of each other's services means students are better served as well.

For many years, ISU's placement center, a Student Affairs function, ably served seniors with resume and interviewing help and other types of placement related assistance. Internships were established by academic departments to provide juniors with work experience and college credit. Somewhat newer, the Co-op Program, which fell under the Academic Affairs Division, placed sophomores and juniors in paid, for-credit work experiences in agencies, businesses, and industries around the country. In the fall of 1985, the Vice President for Student Affairs and the Vice President for Academic Affairs decided to create a comprehensive Career Center, one which would meet students' career needs developmentally rather than according to their class status. A third component, Career Planning, was newly created at this time. It was also decided that the newly formed Career Center would report to the Vice President for Student Affairs. This new service would result in a move to an increasingly more centralized approach to the provision of these various services.

When the Career Center moved to its current location in the Student Services Building in 1987, resources that had been accumulated by the two existing components, Placement Services and Professional Practice Programs, were brought together into one location to form the existing Career Center Library. Both components had collected a variety of materials for use by the populations each served. These materials consisted of books and videos on job search skills; directories of businesses and organizations; various magazines; brochures from towns and cities across the country; vacancy listings; and, the bulk of the collection, employer-produced information (print and video) from business, industry, government and social service organizations and from school districts. In addition, a separate "professional" library was housed in the conference room of the new Career Center. Compiled from staff offices, this collection consisted of career development textbooks, one or two directories and some professional association monographs and journals.

Various staff members assumed responsibility for the newly expanded collection. The library was staffed during some of its operating hours by graduate assistants and student workers under the supervision of the Career Planning staff members. The library staff had to train themselves how to use materials so they, in turn, could train students who came to the library. Since the library was not staffed during all its hours of operation, however, help was not always available. In addition, self-training has its limitations: library staff concentrated on materials of interest, or materials they had observed others use. Many resources went untapped.

New acquisitions were approved by a library committee composed of one staff member from each of the three components. Since committee members were also new to each other and to the idea of a comprehensive Career Center, they knew too little about each area's function to give advice. Delays were inevitable as, for example, the Placement Services representative would need to check back with her colleagues to determine the need for a particular title outside of her subject area. Territoriality also played a role as the components struggled to find their place in the new organization. The library, necessary to everyone, was inevitably part of that struggle.

While this variety of influences accounted for a somewhat unbalanced collection, it was also indicative of the value in which the library had been held by the majority of the Career Center staff. Most of the staff took at least a few minutes to guide the student clients with whom they met to appropriate resources. However, again, because they were not yet familiar with the functions of the other components, counselors were not always familiar with resources they had not brought with them to the new organization.

THE SOLUTION

In the fall of 1987, the Dean of Library Services met with the Career Center Director to discuss the CCL operations and ways to improve its services. After that meeting, several librarians visited the CCL and made a number of recommendations. Better coordination of materials acquisition was strongly encouraged. They also suggested that a LUIS (Library User Information System) terminal be placed in the CCL so its users could find career information available elsewhere on campus. The librarians recommended that CCL materials be cataloged and loaded onto LUIS and that access to employer information be improved by including it on LUIS as well.

Based upon the recommendations of the Dean of Libraries, in May 1988, the Director of the Career Center recommended to the

Vice President for Student Affairs that a full time librarian be hired to manage the Career Center Library. This individual would be a library faculty member assigned to the Career Center and the Student Affairs Division to provide direct student services. It was also agreed that the librarian's salary and benefits be paid by the Student Affairs Division.

Once the proposal received approval, the search process began. In the interim, a temporary support staff person was hired, again funded by Student Affairs, to load the Career Center Library collection into the ISU Libraries NOTIS database. A librarian with professional experience in the student affairs field was hired and assumed the position in December 1988.

IMPLEMENTATION

It has been said of special libraries that their primary goal has to be to provide information access, not just to the immediate collection alone, but to outside resources as well. Access to information becomes more important than mere ownership of information, because then resources are no longer limited to those available in the immediate location.[3] As the Career Center Library developed, it became increasingly clear that it was functioning as a special library, albeit within the parameters of a university setting. The library's goals and objectives flow directly from those of the Career Center, and it actively serves the information needs of the Career Center staff.

The CCL's primary goal is to provide access to information, and it could not accomplish this goal without the support of the ISU Libraries. While the CCL is able to interact with any unit in the main library, it most often draws upon the expertise and services of Acquisitions, Cataloging, Reference, Library Instruction, and Collection Development. The Career Center Library collection is a part of the ISU Libraries' online catalog, LUIS (Library User Information System). ISU Libraries also provides a terminal in the CCL for patron use. Not only is the CCL collection available to all of those who make use of LUIS, but students using the Career Center Library can access other collections on campus as well. Thus, someone searching the catalog for information on resumes would find references to books, software and videos on resumes housed in the Career Center Library, as well as to the resources available at other libraries represented in the catalog. This kind of networking, with the CCL being a satellite of the ISU Libraries, greatly improves service to the students, faculty, alumni, and others who make use of the Career Center and its library.

In developing the objectives necessary to carry out the goals of the Career Center Library it is necessary to gather information about the population served by the CCL through discussions with students, faculty, and staff. This information is helpful in determining the needs and perceptions of potential users. At this time it is important to take advantage of the expertise of the career counselor as a practitioner in his or her field when developing a greater awareness of the kinds of resources that are needed in the area of career development. It is necessary to constantly be made aware of the ephemeral information that is difficult to acquire, such as employer information (annual reports, brochures), and the various career-field specific job listings that are available, and career counselors are very helpful in this area. Keeping this information as current as possible is important both for ease of access and conservation of space, which increasingly becomes an issue as growth continues. In accomplishing these objectives, the career center library functions as an information center which provides highly current, highly specific materials on both the current labor market and the career development process.

INSTRUCTION

Another important factor in accomplishing the goals of the career center library lies in instruction. Teaching people how to use the Career Center Library is an important part of providing access to the information available there. Because of the small size of the library, and its relationship to the career counselors who use the library as a means of support for their own instruction and counseling of students, the way in which the staff is trained in the use of the library will greatly affect the students' perceptions of the library and its services. Initially, training library workers in using the library and in being a bridge between a library user's information need and the library resources available to meet that need is most important. The development of a staff manual which is tailored to address the special problems that arise in this type of library is needed in order to address public service issues and day-to-day policies and procedures.

The career center counselors also need training in the use of the library, although through different means. The counselors greatly influence student perceptions; if they think that the library's resources are useful, they will be sure to communicate this in their counseling sessions. Training them, however, requires delicacy if any of them had influence in the shape, use, or organization of the existing collection, particularly if the library was started without the help of a librarian. Making the staff more aware of the growing potential of the collection through its management by a librarian, an individual whose expertise lies in information access and retrieval, can be done through both informal group and one-on-one discussions. Both of these can be designed to teach counselors to effectively access the collection which they are helping to develop. Sessions designed to help counselors address the needs of a special area are also helpful; for example, finding information helpful to counselors working with liberal arts students who are trying to tap the hidden job market.

DIRECTIONS FOR FUTURE GROWTH

The unique relationship which the CCL has with ISU Libraries has proved to be an effective marketing tool for the Career Center. Students using LUIS to search for materials on career development are drawn to the Career Center and the services it provides. This advertisement of Career Center services also helps to develop important faculty liaisons throughout the campus. Since the CCL librarian is a faculty member, the services the CCL provides are further legitimized to the faculty, and this helps them realize what a vital cornerstone career development is to a university's academic services.

One important facet of promoting the service is tracking progress and recording development. The implementation of surveys can help continually to identify needs, while the recording of statistics can help identify what needs are and are not being satisfied (Figure 1), and to justify what has been achieved by showing progress (Figure 2).

As the Career Center Library continues to expand its resources and services, new available technologies constantly need to be explored. As electronic information needs are identified, the relationship between the CCL and ISU Libraries will become increasingly critical as the possibility of networking electronic services develops and evolves, and as budgetary constraints dictate the sharing of these expensive resources to provide improved student services.

The person selecting and providing information plays a critical role in any organization.[4] In the comprehensive Career Center at ISU, the librarian plays a critical role as a provider of information to the different areas of the center. The CCL exemplifies interdivisional cooperation on a university campus. In addressing the need for better access to career development information, the University Library and the Career Center, each reporting to two different Vice Presidents, set aside their own territorial concerns to develop a cooperative approach in solving this special problem. As a result, students are provided with comprehensive career development information, not just through direct access at the Career Center Library, but by the CCL acting as a bridge to other sources of information which are beyond the confines of the Career Center walls.

FIGURE 1. Career Center Library 1991 Library Survey.

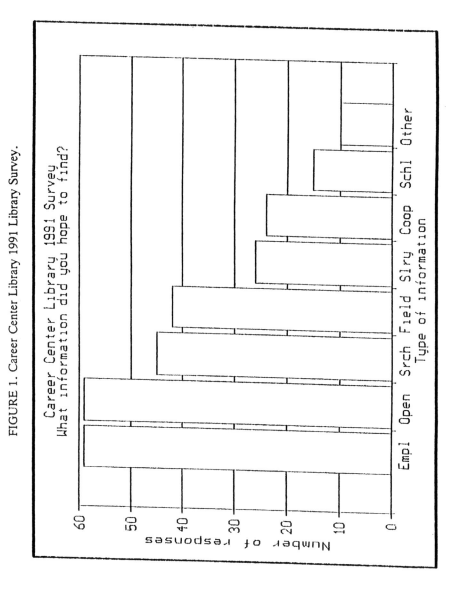

70

Career Center Library 1991 Library Survey

What information did you hope to find here?

```
Graph label:   Type of info:   Responses:
=========================================
Empl           Employers            59
Open           Job Openings         59
Srch           Job Search           45
Field          Career Field         42
Slry           Salaries             26
Coop           Intern/Co-op         24
Schl           School District      15
Other          Other                10
```

Multiple answers: Total >100

FIGURE 2. Career Center Library Annual Patron Count.

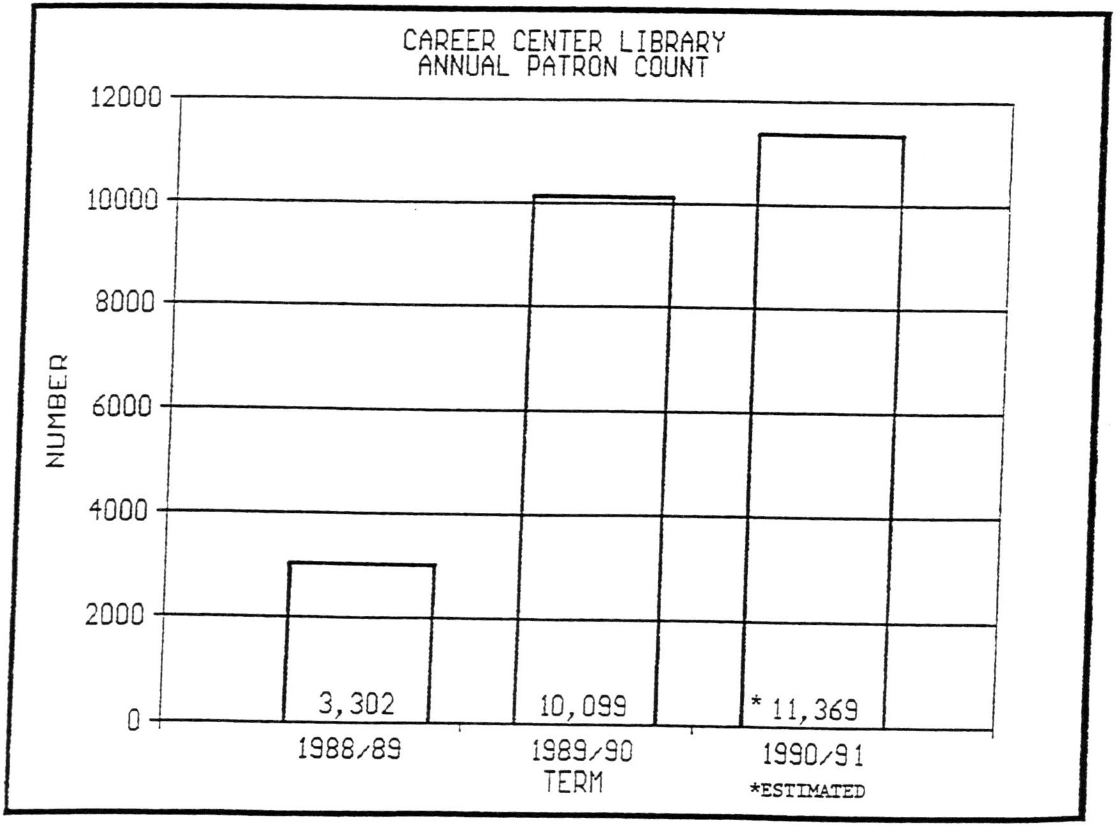

72

CAREER CENTER LIBRARY
ANNUAL PATRON COUNT

	1988/89	1989/90	1990/91
FALL	N/A	3,698	4,756
BREAK	N/A	235	282
SPRING	N/A	5,133	5,231
SUMMER	N/A	1,033	*1,100
TOTAL	3,302	10,099	*11,369
			(+1,270)

*ESTIMATED

REFERENCES

1. White, Herbert S. "The 'Quiet Revolution': A Profession at the Crossroads." *Special Libraries*, Winter 1989, p. 29.

2. Ibid. p. 26.

3. Paskoff, Beth M. "Networks and Networking: How and Why Special Libraries Should be Involved." *Special Libraries*, Spring 1989, p. 95.

4. Regan, Muriel "The Special Librarian as Front Runner: Running Fast, Running Hard, Running Ahead." *Special Libraries*, Spring 1990, p. 93.

Whither the Working Class?
Library Career Planning Service
for Workers in Transition

Martin Elliot Jaffe

SUMMARY. Details and describes the career transition issues facing the American working class as the economy shifts from manufacturing to new technologies and service sector jobs in the 1990's. Descriptions of displaced workers and adults involved in intentional change are presented. Career counseling strategies utilized with blue collar males are presented. A philosophical and pragmatic basis for using the public library as an adult career resource center is described with discussion of counseling techniques and library resources for proactive change. Focus is on the experiences of the Cuyahoga County (Ohio) Public Library's InfoPLACE Adult Career Resource Center.

They're closing down the textile mill and the jobs ain't coming back.

–Bruce Springsteen

America's traditional working class is being profoundly affected as the American economy evolves from traditional manufacturing industries toward new technologies and service based industries. Where can America's blue collar workers in transition find effective vocational planning resources and individualized career counseling as they plan for the vocational challenges of the 1990's and beyond? While Durrance (1991) has recently reviewed public library career services in a broad spectrum of career changers, this essay

Martin Elliot Jaffe is a Career Consultant at the Cuyahoga County Public Library, InfoPLACE Service, 5225 Library Lane, Maple Heights, OH 44137.

75

will identify the issues and responses of library career resource centers as they respond to the needs of the working class population, a group traditionally underserved by the American public library (Estabrook, 1981). Two distinct sub-groups of this population and their library career resource needs will be discussed: displaced workers and workers engaged in the process of "intentional change" (Tough, 1982). The concerns of career counselors are to meet the needs of workers in transition enabling them to successfully engage in self-assessment, develop expertise in career planning principles and job searching strategies, and utilize a wide range of occupational literature.

WHO ARE THE "WORKING CLASS"?

Poets, professors, and social analysts from varied ideological perspectives have written extensively on the question of "middle class" vs. "working class," etc. From the poet's perspective, Carl Sandburg described the working class as people, "where nobody works unless they have to, and they nearly all have to." More analytically, social critic Barbara Ehrenreich defined the working class:

> By "working class" I mean not industrial workers in hard hats but all those people who are not professionals, managers, or entrepreneurs, who work for wages rather than salaries, and who spend their working hours variously lifting, bending, driving, monitoring, inputting, cleaning, providing physical care for others, loading, unloading, cooking, serving, and the like. The working class, so defined, comprises 60 to 70 percent of the U. S. population. (Ehrenreich, 1989, p. 22)

DISPLACED WORKERS–
THE END OF BLUE COLLAR WORK

Displaced workers, defined as individuals who have been laid off from a job and have little or no chance of returning, represent a new challenge to adult career planning personnel. The dimensions of the problem are summarized below:

- By the end of 1980, one-fourth of auto workers had become unemployed. Currently, even as the auto industry has recovered, over-all employment is only at two-thirds of the level of 1980.
- Job opportunities in manufacturing-related occupations will continue to decline. Semi-skilled crafts workers and operators will continue to be replaced by machines. New openings will be in the service sector in maintenance and repair occupations.
- Current and future trends indicate growth in the number of displaced workers.
- While the number of displaced workers is increasing, community resources available to provide assistance will continue to decline during the 1990's.
- Older displaced workers may resist relocation programs. The glut on local housing markets after large layoffs makes moving financially impossible for some.

According to the Bureau of Labor Statistics, about 10.8 million adults lost their jobs from January 1981 to January 1986 because of shutdown, relocation, slack work or elimination of their positions. Here are some further statistics from the same 1986 BLS survey of 5.1 million displaced workers:

- The largest number of displaced workers–about 1.9 million–were previously employed as operators, fabricators or laborers.
- About two-thirds of the displaced workers were men.
- Median job tenure at the time of job loss was 6.6 years.
- About a third of the workers had been on the job 10 years or more.
- Indiana, Illinois, Ohio, Michigan and Wisconsin accounted for 1.1 million displaced workers. In a study from 1986 about 65 percent had been re-employed, compared with about half of a similar group surveyed in 1984.

• In Michigan, auto industry employment fell from 410,000 in 1978, the peak year, to an estimated 314,000 for 1987, according to Donald Grimes, a University of Michigan research economist.

CAREER COUNSELING ISSUES
FOR BLUE COLLAR MALES

The Cuyahoga County Public Library's InfoPLACE Adult Career Resource Center serves a significant number of blue collar males displaced from the industrial settings noted above. A composite of a "typical" displaced worker client would be a male in his mid to late thirties, married, with two to five children, and ethnically of Eastern European, Appalachian, Black or Hispanic background. In addition, he is a homeowner, military veteran, has ten to fifteen years of experience at a steel mill, auto plant, or other industrial setting, and has never contemplated working anywhere else.

Levinson (1978) has clearly defined the challenges faced by these men in their thirties as they refine and re-direct their life choices, values and goals. Occupational success is a key component of life challenges for men in this era which encompasses what Levinson terms the settling down phase. Levinson outlines five possible sequences a man's life can follow during the Settling Down period: (a) advancement within a stable life structure; (b) serious failure or decline within a stable life structure; (c) breaking out: trying for a new life structure; (d) advancement which itself produces a change in life structure; and (e) unstable life structure (p. 150).

InfoPLACE methods are value based. Unemployment has forced the center's clients out of pattern A. The concern is enabling these men to attain C or D and continue a life pattern based on optimal psycho-social satisfaction and integrity. One key element not adequately addressed from a theoretical perspective needs to be understood if effective counseling for these clients is to be implemented. While Levinson (1978) writes extensively of the "ladder," progression up a series of steps in career advancement during the thirties, the concept is not relevant to the life experience of men who have worked in a unionized environment.

Shorris (1981) provides insight on how the effect of the union removes the necessity for blue collar men to compete with each other:

> Wage agreements made through collective bargaining contribute to the class unity of blue collar workers. The knowledge that all men on an assembly line who do similar work earn the same wage eliminates the sense of work as competition, uniting men in far-reaching ways. (p. 145)

Shorris reinforces his point by describing the assembly line as "a place where secrets have no use and no place, for the leveling of unionism and of the line itself relieves men of the need to compete if the workers on the line struggle together against the boss, the working conditions or the work itself" (p. 144).

While unionization used to foster group solidarity and collective identity, the unfortunate reality is that in the new American economy of the 1990's, these displaced workers are competing for positions in an economy where unionization has declined. A recent survey by the AFL-CIO noted:

- At 17 million in 1989, union membership in AFL-CIO affiliated unions and in all others outside the federation was down to about 16 percent of all full-time, nonsupervisory, nonagricultural workers, compared to 35 percent in the years following World War II. Moreover, 80 percent of the decline had occurred since 1960.
- 80 percent of all workers under 35 have no union members in their households.
- In 1980, 47 percent of high school graduates over 25 held union represented employment. By 1988, only 31 percent of high school graduates were in union represented jobs.

The challenge for blue collar men on longterm layoff is to come to grips with painful reality; their jobs are probably gone forever and they will need to assess their past experience, develop a plan for the future, and negotiate a transition they never expected to face. Two interrelated components form the base of InfoPLACE's operational core: individual client assessment and skill-building, and utilization of occupational information and educational training materials. The concept of "empowerment" (Bolles, 1984) is central to InfoPLACE's goals. Empowerment enables clients to gain self-awareness, knowledge of their transferable skills, and competence in utilizing occupational information for effective vocational decision-making now and in the future. Bolles (1980) also has defined the essence of the vocational counseling interview in a series of steps: (1) What does this client perceive his/her problem to be? What do *I* perceive his/her problem to be? (2) Does the client know what transferable skills he/she has and which of these he/she most enjoys and does best? The rest of the steps are concerned with identifying and approaching organizations using the individual's skills and being hired by that organization.

Blue collar workers often have a difficult time in developing an understanding of how their experience in a routinized job can involve transferable skills. They lack self-confidence and self-esteem. InfoPLACE has found that going over an extensive checklist of skill areas with a client is often useful as a method of pinpointing skills. The center has developed extensive skill sort and ranking exercises that are used with a client to familiarize this individual with the concept of transferable skills.

InfoPLACE's clients almost always want to develop a resume, even if they haven't yet defined a new career goal or developed an understanding of how resumes are used. The resume concept is deeply ingrained in the popular consciousness and viewed as a mystical path to a job. InfoPLACE de-mystifies the resume and redefines it as a pragmatic tool. The center will not work on a resume with a client until the self-assessment and goal-setting process has been undertaken.

The resume writing process is quite valuable as an esteem-building exercise for InfoPLACE's clients. Levinson (1978) has described the BOOM (Becoming One's Own Man) Phase of a man's late thirties. Prior to their layoff, clients were generally succeeding in developmental tasks, and becoming more senior members of their community, family and workplace, and speaking with more authority and authenticity. Their self-esteem was shaken when deprived of the self-assurance and dignity that came from being a bread-winner. By working on their resume, clients become aware of the past successes, experience and skills they have developed, which is meant to enable them to succeed again.

Lopez (1983) provides an excellent summary of the pragmatic and philosophical concerns relevant for the career counselor engaged in counseling the displaced worker:

1. Clarifying marketable, transferable work skills, reviewing vocational assessment results, and focusing on developing short-term plans to reorient clients to the reality of their situations.
2. Providing ample opportunities for clients to express their feelings and focusing on vocational and personal concerns.
3. Assessing clients' financial, familial, marital, and other personal support.
4. Providing clients with up-to-date information on referral services, employment outlook, and local placement services.
5. Reminding clients that they are proven, skilled, mature workers whose job losses are not attributable to incompetence or negligence.

INTENTIONAL CHANGE AND THE WORKING CLASS

Displaced workers are only one sector of the American working class in transition. InfoPLACE constantly counsels workers in transition who are engaged in the process of intentional change. InfoPLACE has been on the cutting edge of adult career decision making, educational planning, and job search strategy implementation since 1976. The center is intensively utilized by a demographic and socio-economic cross section of Cuyahoga County adults.

A useful format for understanding the career transition service needs of the adult worker has been developed by Tough (1982). Tough devised a study focused on assessing what interest areas adults choose for intentional changes in their lives. Tough believes that the first element defining an intentional change is choice; the person chooses a particular area and the choice is voluntary, not coerced. The second element of this process is striving or action; the person must take steps to achieve the chosen change. Tough conducted intensive interviews with 150 adults in the United States, Canada and the United Kingdom to assess their intentional changes.

He found intentional changes were focused in four key areas: (1) career, job and training (33 percent); (2) human relations, emotions and self-perception (21 percent); (3) enjoyable activities (11 percent); and (4) residence/location (10 percent). These four areas account for 75 percent of all intentional changes.

WHY CAREER PLANNING IN THE PUBLIC LIBRARY?

Where can the working class find the vocational resource materials and career counseling interventions to aid them in planning for the transitions of the 1990's and beyond? The public library, existing as a resource for the entire community, is the ideal source for a centralized, comprehensive, adult career planning center.

Developing comprehensive skills in the subtle nuances of interpersonal communications has been a traditional concern of libraries for more than one hundred years. In 1876, Samuel Sweet Green of the Worcester (Massachusetts) Public Library presented a paper at a national librarian's conference, and established the philosophical tradition that underlies InfoPLACE's career advisory program of 1991. As Mr. Green said, "A hearty reception by a sympathizing friend, and the recognition of someone at hand who will listen to inquiries" (Quoted in Tarin and Shapiro, 1981, p. 2369).

While much of the intellectual emphasis of library science has recently centered on information technologies and administrative organization, Green's paper underscores a significant point: librarians are human services professionals and share the same intellectual tradition of helping professionals. Both stress the importance of communication and the implementation of communication strategies to enhance goal seeking behavior. Penland (1974) highlighted the functional strategy of the library endeavor through interpersonal communication. He believes that each patron is considered to be a responsible participant in his own growth process not merely a passive receiver of the communicator's advice, information or instruction program.

Fine (1980), Director of the Institute on Career Collections Development and Counseling at the University of Pittsburgh, advocates the role of the librarian as counselor. She states, "While the skills taught at the Institute are fundamental to the counseling profession, they are not the sole prerogative of professional counselors.'' She expands on this statement:

> Career counseling has traditionally been viewed as the prerogative of "career counselors" with professionals trained in specific areas and theories and charged with the professional responsibility to provide career guidance. But a major limitation in the effective delivery of career guidance is that while counseling professionals may be highly skilled in counseling, they are generally untrained and unskilled in handling the vast amounts of information available. (p. 47-48)

Frederickson (1984) discusses ''an embarrassing problem'' for vocational guidance practitioners: the lack of career information materials offered to career counseling clients. He cites numerous surveys to document his assertion. Frederickson states the vital role of career information as an essential component in clarifying and identifying short-term and lifetime goals:

> Career information helps clients to be more specific about their personal goals; aspiration levels are matched with ability assessments; goals are translated into meaningful terms; personal goals are examined in light of the reality of the world of work. (p. 280)

Hoppock (1966) emphasises the central role of accurate, comprehensive occupational information as vital to the career planning process. InfoPLACE follows in the philosophical tradition established by Hoppock, Fine and others.

THE INFOPLACE MODEL

Jeanne M. Patterson, Director of InfoPLACE, Cuyahoga County Public Library System's Adult Career Resource Center, described the primacy of work in adult learning and development. She said,

> As I worked with adults in educational areas, I discovered that nearly any adult who is continuing education is doing so in connection with work. That flew in the face of some earlier

ideas: the theoretical, idealistic view that libraries are full of independent learners seeking the help of librarians to help plan their learning projects. Experience showed that most adults who came to the library for help with either formal or informal learning are usually learning for a purpose in connection with furthering or changing their careers.

Our philosophy is to provide high-quality career services and career information for adults who have no easy access to a career counselor. In addition to our extensive circulating collection of career resource materials, individual appointments with the four person career counseling staff, and group workshops on career planning and job search strategies, Info-PLACE publishes its own widely distributed *Survival Guide* of services for the unemployed and economically disadvantaged, as well as the *Resume Preparation Guide, Career Decision and Job Finding Sourcebook*, and *Community Services Directory and Education Directory of Northeastern Ohio*.

CAREER COUNSELING GOALS FOR WORKERS IN TRANSITION

Career counseling interventions can be richly endowed with the core values of intentional change: freedom, choice, responsibility, and the search for authentic existence as a process of subjective awareness and choice. Homan (1986) explicitly defines the thematic richness of career counseling as an existential process:

Vocation as the quest for authentic existence is fundamentally a dialectical question of "Who am I and who am I to become?" The question is distinct from the common vocational question of "What can I do?" The former question is dialectical because one is always pressed to ask the question and answer it as one is coming into being; it is a dynamic question. The latter question is a static question because one is objectified. (p. 21)

In the career decision workshops and individual counseling sessions, InfoPLACE uses several exercises designed to focus clients toward self generated choices and weighing of value decisions. The locus of control is an issue with intentional choice meanings. How did a career counseling client make an initial career choice? Did he do what family members or significant others told him to do or expected him to do?–(an external locus of control) or did he choose his own path, seek authenticity and accept responsibility for his choice?–(an internal locus of control). The exercise by Jaffe (1988), WHO SAYS–THEY OR I, is designed to introduce clients to the locus of control issue. The thematic flow of the workshop that follows reinforces the dynamic of choice integral to the career planning process and central to the viewpoint of existential career counseling: the individual chooses freedom by accepting one's autonomy, responsibility and choice.

Choosing work values and life values are career counseling themes addressed by Jaffe, Patterson, and Rehor (1988). Two exercises have been designed, MONEY IS EVERYTHING–OR IS IT, a life values choice inventory, and WORK VALUES CARD SORT. Both exercises have clients choose and rank order their values in a dynamic subjective process. Later exercises focus on evaluating specific occupations to assess the relationship of the expressed values to a prospective career. Jaffe (1988) summarized the existential awareness that is at the heart of the career planning choice process:

> Career vision begins with an inner awareness of discontent, a feeling that there is something out there that you want to do and the awareness that you need a plan to reach out and find a path to your goal. Vision provides the energy for career exploration, the motivation to turn inward first and say to yourself, "Self, what are the values, experiences, skills, and life goals at which I want to spend forty or more hours per week?"

CAREER SERVICES FOR WORKERS IN TRANSITION: THE CONTINUING CHALLENGE

The need of the newly unemployed for career counseling was documented by Parsons, Griffore and LaMore (1983). They studied

171 newly unemployed adults in Lansing, Michigan. A survey of their informational needs ranked learning techniques of looking for work as number one in preference. Asked to rank how they preferred to receive information, the respondents expressed a strong preference for workshops and classes on looking for work, job retraining programs, and resume preparation and interviewing skills.

Career counseling for adults in transition is a critical need that will remain vitally important in the challenging and unsettling time ahead. The ongoing challenge for career counselors was summarized by William Pilder, director of a job-hunting skills program for displaced steel workers in Johnstown, Pennsylvania:

> What we have to do is to get people to see themselves in another way–we say put a new frame on yourself. A man may see himself as a millwright, an unemployed millwright, but he has a lot of other skills. Our work is really healing serious depression, healing depressed energies and getting them going. Carl Jung said, "You don't choose change, life steps up and challenges you and either you have the capacity to respond or not." So we're talking about a transformation of the psyche; individuals have to believe they can transform themselves in mid-life–then the collective will move when the individual energy is freed. [Quoted in Smith (1984)]

This ongoing concern will confront us as we face the responsibility of implementing vital and viable education services for the challenging decades ahead. Levine and Piggins (1981) have suggested a comprehensive strategy to ensure success in our collective endeavors:

> Very little will change without a concerted, cooperative effort to create national policy, laws, and appropriations for adult learning projects. There needs to be a national body as well as regional bodies made up of government, labor, industry, education and community representatives that can help to create policy, exchange information, and begin to some intelligent

and realistic planning about how to provide lifelong learning opportunities to create a more dynamic work force and a more informed populace. (p. 27)

REFERENCES

Bolles, R. N. (1980). "A Vest Pocket Guide to Career Counseling." pp. 2-4.

Bolles, R. N. (1984). Presentation delivered at the "Career and Life Planning Workshop." Toronto, June 1984.

Durrance, J. (1991). "Public Libraries and Career Changers: Insights from Kellogg-funded Sources." *Public Libraries*, 30 (2): 93-100.

Ehrenreich, B. (1989). "Working-Class Heroes No More." *Harper's*, 279 (1675): 22, 26-27. Reprint of "The Silenced Majority" in the September 1989 *Z Magazine*.

Estabrook, L. (1981). "Labor and Librarians: the Divisiveness of Professionalism." *Library Journal*, 106 (2): 125-127.

Fine, S., ed. (1980). *Developing Career Information Centers*. New York: Neal-Shumann.

Frederickson, R. H. (1984). "The Value and Use of Career Information." *Vocational Guidance Quarterly*, 32 (4): 277-281.

Homan, K. (1986). "Vocation as the Quest for Authentic Existence," *Career Development Quarterly*, 35 (1): 14-22.

Hoppock, R. (1966). *Occupational Information*. New York: McGraw-Hill.

Jaffe, M. (1988). "Channeling Career Dreams into Plans of Action," *Cleveland Jewish News* (August 26): 32.

Jaffe, M., J. Patterson, and D. Rehor (1988). "Value Exercises/Card Sorts." Cleveland, OH: Cuyahoga County Public Library System, InfoPLACE.

Levine, H. and D. Piggins (1981). "Workplace Counseling: the Missing Link." In: F. Silvestre, ed. *Advising and Counseling Adult Learners*. New York: Jossey-Bass, pp. 19-28.

Levinson, D. J. (1978). *Season's of a Man's Life*. New York: Knopf.

Lopez, F. G. (1983). "The Victims of Corporate Failure: Some Preliminary Observations," *Personnel and Guidance Journal*, 61, pp. 631-632.

Parsons, M. A., R. J. Griffore, and R. L. LaMore (1983). "Identifying the Needs of Newly Unemployed Workers," *Journal of Employment Counseling*, 20, pp. 107-112.

Penland, P. R. (1974). *Interpersonal Communication: Counseling, Guidance and Retrieval for Media, Library and Information Specialists*. New York: M. Dekker.

Shorris, E. (1981). *The Oppressed Middle Politics of Middle Management*. New York: Anchor Press/Doubleday.

Smith, A. (1984). "If 'Smokestack America' Shrinks, Can Psychology Cure the Depression?" *Esquire*, 101 (4): 106.

Tarin P. and P. Shapiro (1981). "Learning, Jobs and the Quality of Life." *Library Journal*, 106 (21): 2365-2369.

Tough, A. (1982). *Intentional Changes: A Fresh Approach to Helping People Change*. New York: Cambridge Book Co.

Libraries and Career Planning and Placement Professionals: Partnerships in Assisting Job Seekers

Bruce Bloom

SUMMARY. The 1990's will see a rapid rate of change in many areas that will impact technology, the economy, and people. One specific area of impact will be the job search process. There will be more people changing jobs and careers. To conduct a successful job search, people need easy access to a variety of job search resources. Public libraries already play a key role in providing these vital resources. To accentuate this role, the idea of a partnership is presented between career planning and placement professionals and libraries. Together these two forces can effectively facilitate the job search process. This extended role will lead public libraries to be a hub or center of extensive networking resources crucial for job seekers. Examples from Illinois public libraries with current job search programs, and one volunteer community-based program, will be featured. Text will revolve around the ideas presented during various job search programs, and quotations of professionals in the field.

INTRODUCTION

The 1990s, because of international events, the economy, and technology will see an increase in the number of times people change jobs and careers. This will require job seekers to have ac-

---

Bruce Bloom is Job Search Skills Trainer at Moraine Valley Community College, Job Placement Center Room, 10900 South 88th Avenue, Palos Hills, IL 60465.

89

cess to timely and accurate data to conduct an effective job search. Public libraries will play a vital role in a person's job search because of the valuable information and resources in their collections. This article will focus on specific job search programs sponsored at public libraries in the greater Chicago area.

SKOKIE PUBLIC LIBRARY

The Skokie Public Library began their involvement in job search programs in 1986 when they sponsored two sessions entitled, "The Librarians Review on Job Search" and "Self-employment," presented by reference librarians Steve Oserman and Hope Apple. "One reason we created this workshop was to meet the overwhelming increase in requests for job/career information. Our workshop focuses on reference services available to the general public and teaches individuals how to utilize our services," explained Apple.[1] Apple addressed the incentives and complications behind self-employment with an emphasis on a woman's role in this field placing special focus on freelancing. She said, "Many people have been forced into self-employment because baby boomer adults have saturated the job market and large corporations have been reducing staff."[2]

During his presentation, Oserman discussed how understanding the psychology of success is needed to maintain a positive attitude during the often grueling job search process, and to create a positive rapport with networking contacts and perspective employers. "In order to have a successful interview people need to develop deeper insights into themselves, be aware of other types of people, and use direct communication," Oserman informed. Self-help books on cognitive psychology, such as two titles by David D. Burns, *Feeling Good: The New Mood Therapy* (New York: Morrow, 1980) or *Intimate Connections* (New York: Morrow, 1985), help people become aware of the stress involved in going through a job search and effectively deal with it. He went on to emphasize, "Another excellent resource for the job search is the stock market because information on stocks and the direction the market is moving can be used to explore potential areas of growth and change. People do not want to enter a career that has no potential for development. Think of the stock market as a barometer to indicate changes and directions within the business environment."[3]

Since 1988, the library has sponsored three free job search lectures featuring Marilyn Moates Kennedy, author of several job search books, as the keynote speaker. Kennedy emphasized, "The key to a successful job search is to figure out what you have to sell, and concentrate on finding organizations that value what you do well. This will achieve the objective of a good fit between you and the organization." She added, "you must discover what you want to sell and find a company that is looking for that image."[4] Commenting on the prolific job creations of smaller companies, Kennedy stressed, "People should be focusing on small to medium size companies listed in *Venture* and *Inc* magazines instead of exhausting their energy on the Fortune 500."[5] She further noted that when interviewing, job hunters need to ask three things:

> When was my predecessor promoted?
> What qualities other than skills, experience, and education are necessary to succeed in this job?
> Please describe a typical day.

Other topics addressed that day were: Interviewing; Decision Making; Career Changes; Winning Skills; How to Find a Job in Chicago; Job Search; and Job Search and the Older Worker. All of these programs presented material that job seekers could use to increase the effectiveness of their job search.

Another benefit Skokie has to offer the job seeker is the networking opportunities found following the formal workshop presentations. Participants would stay to ask questions of the presenters, and exchange job search information with others. Many referrals were made.

COOK MEMORIAL LIBRARY

Cook Memorial Library in Libertyville, Illinois, has sponsored two job search seminars presented by consultant Robert H. Wilcox.

Wilcox presented material meant to help people conduct an effective and productive job search. He emphasized, "Accomplishments on a resume are what you do at work, enjoy doing, do well, and are proud of. When leaving a job there are three reasons: the real reason, the organization's reason, and the reason you and the employer agree on."[6]

Wilcox stressed four points on interviewing: preparation, practice, listening, and follow up. He said,

> Interviewers look for people with enthusiasm and positive attitude, problem solving capability, articulate, confident, poised, broad-based background and specific communication skills. In preparation for an interview, research the organization, the job, and the interviewer; prepare answers to questions they will ask; identify key qualifications; establish your objective for the interview; and plan your physical presentation (clothes, haircut and cosmetics). When interviewing keep answers brief and concise, and include concrete quantifiable data. Repeat your key strength three times and prepare five or more success stories. Put yourself on their team—image is often as important as content. Ask questions and maintain conversation. Plan—research the company, products, lines and competitors, and follow up.[7]

SCHAUMBURG TOWNSHIP PUBLIC LIBRARY

The Schaumburg Township Public Library, Schaumburg, Illinois, hosted a Self Help Employment Development Program (SHED) for over thirty people in 1987. They forged a unique partnership with the Catholic Charities' successful SHED program. This partnership came about because of conversations between SHED graduate Tom Duszynski and Barbara Adrianopoli, Head of Extension Services for the library. Duszynski, who used the library's resources while between jobs, strongly believed the program was a positive force in his life and job search.

At the first session, Robert Frankel, Library Board President, stressed, "The hardest job you have is to find a job, but by attending this program you are off to a tremendous start." He added, "People starting out today will change positions, companies and careers four or five times during their working lives."[8]

SHED Program Director Rita Oster explained, "The program focuses on sharing experiences, ideas, networking, and discovering your strengths and weaknesses through active participation."[9] The workshop consisted of ten sessions of four hours each. When the participants completed the workshop they received a certificate of achievement and formed a job support group called In Between Jobs which held weekly meetings at the library.

Tom Malouf, consultant, facilitated another one of the sessions. He emphasized, "When you are changing careers you need a plan and a process for career choice," and added, "You must look at your skills, abilities, values, likes and dislikes about previous jobs, and your successes and failures to determine your future direction."[10] Malouf strongly believed that objective data from Myers-Briggs and Strong Campbell interest inventories, along with an individual's own subjective data from self-assessment testing, gives a person the opportunity to create options in possible career paths to pursue.

CHICAGO PUBLIC LIBRARY

At the Chicago Public Library, Career Reference Librarian Jerry Husfeldt stressed, "There are three types of basic users in the Center: those seeking company information for interviews; those trying to put together a list of possible potential employers and industries for targeting their resumes; and those looking for tips on choosing careers." Husfeldt further commented, "These patrons come together to a central point which has books on a variety of job related topics, including career fields, interviewing, resumes, choosing a place to work, and test preparation. The Center also has a bulletin board with timely pieces of advice and article clippings on job search topics."[11]

The purposes of the Chicago Public Library's career workshops are to: encourage an awareness of the variety of available resources; encourage an awareness of the kinds of questions that reference librarians should be asked; help participants to understand that competition for employment is great and this workshop may assist them to obtain a competitive edge on the average job hunter; and to understand that job seekers in general are increasingly becoming more sophisticated out of necessity.

Some of the objectives of the workshop were to:

1. distinguish the difference between a company and an industry;
2. know what it means for a company to be publicly-held as opposed to privately-held;
3. know what a company plant is and where to find company plant information for the Chicago area;
4. know the major divisions of the Career Information Center;
5. define a trade journal;
6. know the value of research and reflection in choosing a career;
7. locate books that list companies under specific industry categories; and
8. know sources for locating information on publicly-held companies and specific industries.

A partial list of topics presented at the job search seminar were: How to Find a Job in Chicago; Women Employed on the Inside Track; Job Hunting for the 90's; Future of the American Workplace; and, How to make $1,000 a Minute: Secrets of Negotiating Salary Increases and Raises.

LAKE FOREST CAREER RESOURCE CENTER

The Career Resource Center in Lake Forest, Illinois, is free to job seekers and employers. It is funded by a local church and staffed by volunteers who have a background in career counseling, personnel and job placement. The purpose of the organization is to help meet the needs of members in the community who are unemployed, anticipating unemployment, changing careers or jobs, re-entering the job market due to a change in a life situation, and recent college graduates.

Some of the services offered are:

- professional career counseling seminars;
- assistance in preparing professional and effective resumes;
- training in using numerous job hunting and job reference sources;
- training in using various job hunting techniques, especially the networking process;
- training in effective interviewing techniques and practice interviewing;
- use of the center's work spaces, literature, bulletins, telephones, job listings, etc.; and
- continuing support throughout the job search process as needed.

The Career Resource Center has a monthly job support group. Gerry Aiuppa, Career Placement Manager at Oakton Community College, believes that support groups are a critical part of the job search process: "Many unemployed seek job support groups to affirm their self-worth and build confidence to get back on the job track. The unplanned time off from work could be used to gain new skills, retrain for possible career changes, and to gain a competitive edge which offers people the chance for self-renewal and personal growth."[12]

Another critical part of the job search process, according to Aiuppa, is networking. She emphasized, "Another alternative to advertised listings is to consult with friends, relatives, former employers, acquaintances, peers, professional organizations, and anyone remotely aware of potential job vacancies to build a network of "information brokers." In a competitive market, "contacts" is the name of the game with most judgment jobs rewarded to people who work through targeted people."[13]

CONCLUSION

These are examples of practical job search programs that libraries have tried and found successful. Public libraries should have these types of programs on an on-going basis. Job seekers should not have to wait for economic conditions to slow down before programs are offered in effective job search skills. Programs and workshops can be developed using natural partnerships between public libraries and job search professionals. This not only provides the job seeker two excellent resources, but also markets the services of the library in a significant way. It is a cost effective way to present programs that are win/win for everyone involved.

REFERENCES

1. Quoted in Bloom, Bruce, "Potpourri of Job Search Info Available to Public," *Chicagoland Job Source* (October 27, 1986): p. 4.

2. Ibid.

3. Ibid.

4. Quoted in Bloom, Bruce, "Smaller Companies Offer Best Bets for New Jobs," *Chicagoland Job Source* (June 20, 1988): p. 4.

5. Ibid.

6. Quoted from memo from Sharon Katterman, Moraine Valley Community College, to Bruce Bloom regarding the Job Search Seminar presented by Robert H. Wilcox, Cook Memorial Library, Libertyville, Illinois (December 30, 1990).

7. Ibid.

8. Quoted in Bloom, Bruce, "Programs Provide Job Search Resources and Group Support," *Chicagoland Job Source* (May 18, 1988): p. 4.

9. Ibid.

10. Malouf, Thomas, "Assessing Your Career," workshop handout, Schaumburg Township Public Library (January 24, 1991).

11. Quoted in Bloom, Bruce, "Libraries Expand Career Resources for Job Seekers," *Chicagoland Job Source* (August 10, 1987): p. 4.

12. Aiuppa, Gerry, "Job Coping Strategies in Uncertain Times," *Career Corner*, 15, no. 17 (January 15, 1991): p. 16.

13. Ibid.

Career Information:
One Library's Services

Beth Ann Krohler
Cecelia R. Howard

SUMMARY. An abundance of material in numerous formats exists which provides information on schools, careers, and jobs. Regardless of the economic climate, demand for this information and service is always present. This chapter discusses the career/job sources and services provided at the Muncie Public Library. Included are issues of currency, authority, and the direction of program and services.

INTRODUCTION

Regardless of the economic climate, demand for school, career, and job information sources are always present. The people who request the information range from children to senior citizens. Libraries are often expected to provide a wide variety of information for various age and reading levels, occasionally requiring multiple copies, in addition to having the capability of accessing various formats. Examples of questions that this information could address or might be asked of a librarian include: What information do you have about this career/school? Do you have any information about this company? Where is financial aid available? How do I write a resume? Do you have a study book for this _____ test? How can I start my own business? How do I look for a job? What schools

Beth Ann Krohler is the Special Projects Librarian and Cecelia R. Howard is the Young Adult/Career Librarian at the Muncie Public Library, Muncie, IN 47305.

97

offer a degree in _____? Answers to these and other questions come from books, college catalogs, periodicals, newspapers, audio-visual material, computer software, and people. This information can become outdated quickly, so frequent updating is necessary. Whether a library has a special centralized collection or an integrated collection, work is necessary to maintain relevancy.

MATERIALS SELECTION

The Muncie Public Library provides a centralized collection of material on careers, schools, financial aid, job hunting, resumes, and test study books at its Main Library. Locating the material in a designated area affords ease of use and makes for efficient use of staff time. Adequate signage lends visibility to the collection. In addition to the careers/jobs collection, a few broad, general items are kept in the Reference Collection. The library maintains a separate Business and Technical Collection where material on starting and running a business is kept. At the Main Library's Adult Education Collection, material purchased for the new reader is maintained. Each of the branch libraries, children's areas, and Audiovisual Center also maintain materials on career and job subjects for various age levels.

Material is selected by several professional staff members. The centralized career collection materials (for all ages) is selected by the Young Adult Librarian. Material for each of the other areas mentioned above is selected by appropriate librarians. As with any material purchased, several criteria are considered, for instance, need, currency, comprehensiveness, authority, price, organization, and reading level.

An abundance of material is available concerning schools, careers, and jobs. Keeping current can be overwhelming. Some publishers have a reputation for excellence in these fields and material is ordered from them without concern. In some cases this is done with a standing order through the publisher or jobber. By using this method, the library is assured of timely receipt of this material without having to go through an order process each time. Publishers in this category include:

- Arco Publishing, Inc., Div. of Prentice-Hall, 15 Columbus Circle, New York, NY 10023
- Barron's Educational Series, Inc., P. O. Box 8040, 250 Wireless Blvd., Hauppauge, NY 11788
- Peterson's Guides, Inc., P. O. Box 2123, Princeton, NJ 08543-2123
- Rosen Publishing Group, Inc., 29 E. 21st St., New York, NY 10010
- VGM Career Horizons, National Textbook Co., 4255 W. Touhy Ave., Lincolnwood, IL 60646-1975
- National Learning Corporation, 212 Michael Dr., Syosset, NY 11791.

The *National Job Bank* and the Job Bank Series published by Bob Adams, Inc., 260 Center St., Holbrook, MA 02343-1074, is useful for information on major employers by industry and geographic area.

Some publishers issue a series of pamphlet material on a regular basis. Examples include:

- Careers, Inc., P. O. Box 135, Largo, FL 34649
- The Institute for Research, Box 8039A, Northfield, IL 60093
- Chronicle Guidance Publications, Inc., P. O. Box 1190, Moravia, NY 13118-11990.

Several of these publishers also sell mailing labels with professional association addresses to use in requesting free and inexpensive material; however, the Muncie Public Library creates its own labels using an assortment of sources for the addresses. Sources for addresses include material from the above publishers, in addition to the *Encyclopedia of Associations* (1991), *Professional Careers Sourcebook: an Information Guide for Career Planning* (1990), and *Job Hunter's Sourcebook* (1991).

Historically, college catalogs were requested directly from the schools. At Muncie Public Library this is true for schools in Indiana, service academies, and other select schools. Due to a lack of building space, staff time, and the charge for some college catalogs, the staff initially purchased the Career Guidance Foundation's (8090

Engineer Rd., San Diego, CA 92111) catalogs on microfiche; however, a decision was made not to acquire this set every year due to
its cost and limited use. Now the library uses the Micrologue College Catalogs on Microfiche (Micrologue, P. O. Box 2260, Boulder,
CO 80306). This service does not require an index and is easier to
use than the Career Guidance Foundation microfiche. Catalogs on
microfiche are good for looking up specific information, but difficult to read in their entirety. Another drawback, printing microfiche
is expensive.

Aside from ordering from publishers known for their material on
schools, careers, and jobs, MPL uses a variety of review sources.
These include standard titles, such as *Library Journal, School Library Journal, Booklist, Kirkus Review, Kliatt, VOYA,* and *The
Book Report,* as well as less known titles, such as *Career Opportunities News.* Also, material has been selected from traditional library
tools, such as the *Public Library Catalog, The Book Review Index,*
publishers catalogs, and *Books in Print.* A more recent product,
Books in Print Plus is a CD-ROM that combines the print version
of *Books in Print* plus reviews from library periodicals. OCLC or
EPIC can be searched for new editions or subject material. Information about new editions can also be tracked by keeping a file that
indicates the approximate month in which an update is expected to
be available. Finally, material may be purchased or acquired based
on the recommendations of the library's patrons.

Besides using these methods or tools for determining additions
to the careers/jobs collection, several works have become standards
in the MPL library. They include the most recent editions of *Occupational Outlook Handbook* (1990/1991), *Encyclopedia of Careers
and Vocational Guidance* (1990), and *Dictionary of Occupational
Titles* (1991 Rev. ed.).

ADULT PROGRAMS AND SERVICES

Muncie Public Library has, for a long time, placed an emphasis
on providing school, career, and job information to adult users. In
1981, the library received the first American Library Association's
John Sessions Memorial Award given for Project MUNCIE (Mun-

cie UNemployment Community Information Effort). The Project established, with business, labor, and government, a central location staffed by volunteers to disseminate information to the unemployed. The library's bookmobile made stops at several factories. A community forum panel discussion was presented on how to cope with unemployment. The library's Audiovisual Center purchased material on job information and established a viewing area.

When computers entered MPL, one of the first encounters was a service called TEDS (Training and Educational Data Service). This service, created in Indiana, was based on the Guidance Information Systems. Through its files, information was made available on occupations, job training, financial aid, and military careers. For a time, it was heavily used, and required a trained staff member to operate. Some patrons required more counseling than library staff could provide, and these individuals were referred to other organizations.

Computer programs have improved over time. The library now has a product called COIN, created by the Coordinated Occupational Information Network (COIN Education Products, Executive Parkway, Suite 202, Toledo, OH 43606). This very user friendly system does not require a staff member to operate. It allows the patron to access national information on careers and school subjects, occupations, the military, apprenticeships, and colleges. Indiana data includes the Adult Basic Education Centers, private trade schools, and vocational and technical courses and schools. A unique feature is the College Letter Writer that allows a person to format a letter of inquiry to a school. This system is available in hard disk, floppy disk, through networking, CD-ROM, microfiche, and online retrieval.

All computer programs have drawbacks. First, they must be used in the library, even though the information can be printed and taken out. Second, the equipment must be maintained, and it occasionally breaks down. On the other hand, computerization allows for more frequent updates; the software is getting easier to use; and the information and material can be manipulated to suit a particular person or need.

From 1987-1989, the library was able to offer career counseling through a grant. The grant provided a career guidance counselor from a local vocational school. Evening and Saturday appointments were made and the guidance counselor met with patrons at the Main Library or one of the four branch libraries. The service was free and even used by some high school and college students who were uncertain of their career path. The service was more heavily used by older adults who were laid off from their jobs, and by those interested in changing careers.

A career change was once viewed as an admission of failure, but is now a likely fact of life. Much fear and anxiety surrounds change, and the library staff is pleased to be able to help patrons at this crucial time in their lives. Staff members help patrons plan their career changes, deal with their fears, weigh the positives and negatives of changes, and prepare them for a new job search.

Several sessions for unemployed adults have been held at the local employment office by the Indiana Employment Security Division. The Young Adult/Career Librarian spoke to the groups of approximately thirty five people. Those in attendance were most interested in out of town newspapers, telephone books, and Job Bank books to help put them in touch with potential employers in other cities and states. People who were not regular library users were both surprised and pleased with the many materials available. A bibliography entitled, "Books to Help You Find a Job," was given to each person in attendance. Although the seminars were held away from the library, many of those in attendance came to the library during the next few days.

YOUNG ADULT PROGRAMS AND SERVICES

Each summer, the young Adult/Career Librarian works with the Delaware-Blackford Employment Training group at the Indiana Employment Office. This is a summer youth program for economically disadvantaged students, ages 14-21, who are still in school. There has been a total of 350 to 500 students in either classroom training or working at summer jobs. These students are taught how to fill out applications, interview, dress properly, and behave in the workplace.

A sampling of books from the Career Collection on various jobs which might interest teens is taken to the classroom at the Indiana Employment Office. Books on resume writing and interviewing are also included. A bibliography, which includes books, video tapes, and newspapers is given to each student.

A few days after the initial presentation, a tour of the library is arranged for small groups of approximately ten students and two instructors. At that time library skills instruction is given; however, special emphasis is put on the college and career areas and students are taught to use the career encyclopedias, career vertical files, and how to locate information on colleges or vocational schools that might interest them.

The goal is to teach these students some library skills that will make them feel more comfortable and at ease in the library. Staff always tries to emphasize the fact that if students can't find what they're looking for, they should feel free to ask the reference librarian for help.

The Young Adult/Career Librarian also helped local Girl Scout leaders conduct workshops in which Girl Scouts earned a Books Badge. As a part of this badge, the girls were introduced to the College and Career Collection. They were shown how to use the career encyclopedias, career vertical files and college catalogs. Although the emphasis was on career materials, a tour of the library was given. This tour introduced the fifth and sixth graders to the young adult materials, and each girl was given a colorful bookmark. Many came away feeling that the library was a friendly place to read, do homework, or study.

CONCLUSION

The Muncie Public Library is deeply committed to providing information and services concerning schools, careers, and jobs. The activities and ideas mentioned are ones that the MPL have tried in an attempt to provide career and job information. The services are ongoing, though the activities vary. A priority is placed on the marketing of these services. Library newsletters are one method of publicity. Media is another. For instance, information about the materials and programs is sent to the local newspapers, radio and televisions stations, etc. Other publicity methods include bookmarks, bibliographies, signs, brochures, and speaking engagements. The Muncie Public Library staff is constantly trying to evaluate its existing programs and explore new and different ways to meet patron needs.

REFERENCES

Burek, Deborah M., ed. *Encyclopedia of Associations*. New York: Gale, 1991. Annual.

Career Opportunity News. Garrett Park, MD: Garrett Park Press. Bi-monthly.

Hopke, William E., ed. *Encyclopedia of Careers and Vocational Guidance*, 4 vols., 8th ed. Chicago: J. G. Ferguson, 1990.

LeCompte, Michelle, ed. *Job Hunter's Sourcebook*. Detroit, MI: Gale, 1991.

Savage, Kathleen M., and Charity Anne Dorgan, eds. *Professional Career Sourcebook*. Detroit, MI: Gale, 1990.

U. S. Department of Labor. *Dictionary of Occupational Titles*, 2 vols., 4th ed. rev. Washington, DC: Government Printing Office, 1991.

U. S. Department of Labor. *Occupational Outlook Handbook, 1990/91*. Washington, DC: Government Printing Office. Bi-ennial.

III. CAREER AND JOB INFORMATION: EVALUATION AND SOURCES

Evaluating Occupational Information for Use in Libraries and Career Resource Centers

Alan J. Farber

SUMMARY. Occupational information plays a central role in the process of personal career exploration and decision-making. The proliferation, popularity, and high cost of printed, computerized and videotaped occupational information require librarians to assess the material's value prior to purchase and following its use. Fortunately, a number of resources and professional guidelines exist to assist in this endeavor. This chapter describes those factors that need to be taken into account, and the resources available to facilitate the evaluation of occupational information for use in libraries and career resource centers.

INTRODUCTION

The librarian who provides patrons with occupational information is faced with the formidable task of selecting from among a myriad

Alan J. Farber is Coordinator of Career Services at the Counseling and Student Development Center, Northern Illinois University, DeKalb, IL 60115.

of printed, audiovisual and computer-assisted programs and materials available from private vendors, professional associations, the government, educational institutions, and elsewhere. Career materials take many forms, including occupational descriptions; self-help decision-making and job-hunt workbooks; educational, training, and industrial directories; classified advertisements; information about apprenticeships, internships, and volunteer work.

This article is concerned with those materials that can be classified as "occupational information." According to Isaacson (1986) occupational information is "information that is directly concerned with duties, requirements for entrance, conditions of work, rewards, patterns of advancement, and worker supply and demand in various occupations. . . . Simply put, occupational information consists of facts about jobs" (p. 207).

METHODS AND CRITERIA

We are all exposed to a barrage of occupational information on a daily basis in a variety of forms, including encounters with people from a wide array of occupational fields, occupations depicted in the popular media, and occupational information contained within educational coursework. Career resource centers, commonly housed in libraries, high schools, colleges, and businesses, serve as the focal point of career development activities–one of which is obtaining accurate and up-to-date occupational information.

The professional literature is replete with articles detailing the design and implementation of career resource centers (e.g., American Library Association, 1985; Brown & Brown, 1990; Lary, 1985; Minor, 1984; Zunker, 1990), and the organization and classification of occupational information and other career material (e.g., Clack, 1979; Green, 1979). The means of evaluating occupational information, however, has received less attention. Indeed, career material is often selected strictly on the basis of affordability, similarity to materials used in comparable sites, attractiveness of titles, and/or claims and testimonials appearing in publishers' catalogs. The purpose of this article is to provide the librarian with more sensible and systematic criteria with which to appraise career material.

Because the librarian may choose to personally evaluate occupational information or rely on the expertise of other career development specialists, two pre-purchase methods are available. One may either examine the reviews of occupational information contained within professional periodicals and journals, or undertake one's own evaluation using existing professional guidelines produced expressly for that purpose. Whichever method is elected, the decision-maker will necessarily evaluate and select material based on criteria unique to his or her particular situation, taking such factors into account as budget, target population, space, equipment, and availability of support staff.

In his discussion of the evaluation of occupational information, Isaacson (1986) advised that material be measured against the following criteria: accuracy, currency, usability, reader appeal, and comprehensiveness. Hoppock (1976) suggested that the appraiser of occupational literature ask five journalistic questions: "When?" (referring to the material's currency), "Where?" (addressing its geographical limitations), "Who?" (regarding the author's credentials), "Why?" (identifying the material's purpose, such as entertainment, recruitment, or accurate presentation of the facts), and "How?" (pertaining to the manner in which facts were collected and presented).

PUBLICATIONS AND ASSOCIATIONS: REVIEWS AND GUIDELINES

Taking these and other criteria into account, several periodicals and newsletters regularly provide reviews of new career titles: *The Career Planning and Adult Development Newsletter* (Career Planning and Adult Development Network, 4965 Sierra Rd., San Jose, CA 95132, monthly, $40 annual network membership and subscription); *The Career Opportunity News* (Garrett Park Press, Garrett Park, MD 20896, bi-monthly, $30 annual subscription); *Library Journal* (PO Box 1977, Marion, OH 43305-1977, 21 annual issues, $74 annual subscription); and *School Librarian* (PO Box 1978, Marion, OH 43305-1978, monthly, $63 annual subscription).

The Journal of Career Planning and Employment (College Placement Council, 62 Highland Ave., Bethlehem, PA 18017, quarterly, $65 nonmember annual subscription) is published by the College Placement Council whose membership consists primarily of college and university career development specialists, and employers in business, industry and government. *JCPE* articles cover such topics as career centers, career planning, college/corporate relations, computerized systems, occupational outlook, interviewing, and job search strategies. Included in each edition of *JCPE* is the "New Resources" section which consists of one paragraph descriptions of 15-20 recently published career publications. An additional section entitled "Career Media" includes independent reviews of 10-15 books, audiovisuals, and software. Thus, each edition of *JCPE* provides the reader with descriptions and reviews of approximately 30 recent titles of interest to career development specialists.

The American Association of Counseling and Development (5999 Stevenson Ave., Alexandria, VA 22304) is a 58,000 member organization of professionals in a variety of social service fields. One of the AACD's fourteen divisions, the National Career Development Association (formerly the National Vocational Guidance Association) publishes the *Career Development Quarterly* (National Career Development Association, 5999 Stevenson Ave., Alexandria, VA 22304, quarterly, $20 nonmember annual subscription). Each June edition contains the "Current Career Literature" section consisting of ratings of approximately 450 career books, briefs, and pamphlets. The review of these materials falls under the purview of NCDA's Career Information Review Service (CIRS). The CIRS reviewers adhere to the latest revision of the *Career Information Print Materials Review Guidelines* (NCDA, 1991a).

The publications listed in the "Current Career Literature" section are classified according to the following system adopted from Kirk and Michaels (1964):

1. Vocational
   A. Occupations.
   B. Trends and Outlooks.
   C. Job Training.
   D. Employment.

2. Educational
   A. Status and Trends.
   B. Schools, Colleges and Universities.
   C. Scholarships, Fellowships, and Loans.
3. Personal
   A. Planning (resume, job search, etc.).
   B. Adjustment.

The majority of the publications fall into the 1.A. (Vocational, Occupations) category and are evaluated according to the following guidelines (with abbreviated details in parentheses):

General Guidelines

1. Dating and revisions (revisions recommended at least every three to four years).
2. Credits.
3. Accuracy of information (accurate, up-to-date, free from distortion).
4. Format (clear, concise, and interesting).
5. Vocabulary (appropriate to target group).
6. Use of information (purpose, target audience and potential use of the information identified).
7. Free from bias and stereotyping (on the basis of disability, race, gender, social status, ethnicity, age, or religion).
8. Graphics (if used, should enhance publication).

Content Guidelines

1. Duties and nature of work (e.g., purpose of the work, work activities, special competencies).
2. Work setting and conditions.
3. Preparation required (e.g., length and type of training, entry methods).
4. Special requirements for consideration (e.g., license, certification, degrees, memberships, physical requirements, personal criteria, social and psychological criteria).
5. Methods of entering (typical, preferred, alternative means).

6. Earnings and other benefits (figures should be current and represent range).
7. Usual advancement possibilities (e.g., typical and alternative career progressions, supplementary skills and competencies needed).
8. Employment outlook (short and long-range).
9. Opportunities for experience and exploration (e.g., part-time, summer, internships, apprenticeships, volunteer work, etc.).
10. Related occupations.
11. Sources of additional information.

Each publication is rated "Highly Recommended" (maximum adherence to NCDA Guidelines), "Recommended" (general adherence to NCDA Guidelines), or "Useful" (limited in scope, does not adhere to NCDA Guidelines but contains authentic, objective, timely, and helpful information). Publications over two years old or rated "Not Recommended" are not listed in the journal.

In 1987, the W.K. Kellogg Foundation began funding the Public Library Association to help support the development of Education Information Centers (EICs) in public libraries (Public Library Association, 1989). The career-related material and services offered through EICs are particularly geared to traditional non-user groups. In 1989, the EIC Project published an *Annotated Bibliography of the "Best of the Best" Career Books* briefly describing over 70 individual publications and career series deemed particularly useful by a consensus of the staff of public library-based EICs.

Annually since 1972, the National Diffusion Network of the Department of Education (555 New Jersey Ave., Washington, DC 20208-5645) has published *Educational Programs That Work*. This resource, of particular interest to school librarians, is divided into twelve sections containing descriptions of educational programs that have been approved for national dissemination by the federal Joint Dissemination Review Panel (prior to 1987) or the Program Effectiveness Panel (during or after 1987). A positive endorsement is received when a majority of panel members determine that the program provides evidence for cognitive and affective gains. The Career/Vocational Education section of *Educational Programs That Work* contains one-page descriptions of career development programs for implementation in primary to post-secondary educational settings. These programs either incorporate or are used in conjunction with occupational material favorably evaluated by the panel members.

The Educational Resources Information Center (ERIC), a nationwide information network managed by the U.S. Department of Education's Office of Educational Research and Improvement, is designed to provide users with access to education literature. One of ERIC's sixteen clearinghouses, the *Clearinghouse on Adult, Career, and Vocational Education* (Center on Education and Training for Employment, The Ohio State University, 1900 Kenny Rd., Columbus, OH 43210), provides information on career education, including career awareness, career development, career change, and experience-based education. All material submitted to ERIC is evaluated by subject specialists according to the following criteria: (a) contribution to knowledge, significance; (b) relevance; (c) new applications of knowledge, innovative practices; (d) effectiveness of presentation, thoroughness of reporting; (e) responsiveness to current priorities; (f) timeliness; (g) authority of author, source, sponsor; and (h) audience, comprehensiveness (i.e., the size of the audience for which the material is designed).

In addition to disseminating information on the aforementioned topics, ACVE publishes a monthly *ERIC Digest* containing information on such career-related topics as labor market information, career decision-making, and locating job information. The *Digests* often include brief descriptions of directories, workbooks, career guides, and other career-related resources.

VIDEO CAREER MEDIA

Although films, audiotapes and slides have historically been popular career media, videotapes have supplanted their use in many career resource centers, schools, and libraries. This burgeoning popularity of videotaped occupational information served as an incentive for the NCDA's Career Information Review Service to produce a separate set of standards entitled *Guidelines for the Preparation and Evaluation of Video Career Media* (NCDA, 1991b).

Although the NCDA is not currently engaged in the published ratings of videotapes, the guidelines provide a valuable heuristic to those selecting, evaluating or producing videotapes. The NCDA *Video Production and Review Service Evaluation Form* provides a means of scoring each of the following eighteen items on a 3-point scale (0 = Unsatisfactory, 1 = Satisfactory, 2 = Excellent), generating scores of Superior (30-36), Excellent (23-29), Good (16-22), Useful (9-15), and Does Not Meet NCDA Guidelines (0-8). Those items are:

Content

1. Early presentation of intent.
2. Integrity of title.
3. Free of extraneous, noncareer related material.
4. Accurate and adequate presentation of concepts and information.
5. Stimulates transition from passive to active response.

Production Considerations

1. Credits.
2. Picture Quality.
3. Sound Quality.
4. Length.
5. Packaging.

User's Guide

1. Credits.
2. Purpose, objective, and audience.
3. Synopsis.
4. Verifiable results of field testing.
5. Discussion, activities, and resources.

Bias-Free Presentation

1. Free of sex/age role stereotyping.
2. Free of ethnic/race/religious stereotyping.
3. Free of value judgments, social class bias, and self-serving or promotional purposes.

In response to studies demonstrating that nationwide vocational programs were inadequately meeting current and projected manpower needs, legislation was passed in 1976 creating the National Occupational Information Coordinating Committee (NOICC, Suite 156, 2100 M St., NW, Washington, DC 20037) and State Occupational Information Coordinating Committees (SOICCs). The legislation charged the committees to (a) develop and implement a standardized occupational information system to serve the needs of vocational education and employment and training programs at the local, state, and federal levels, and (b) improve coordination and communication among and between the developers and users of occupational information (Flanders, 1988). Librarians interested in arranging demonstrations from their statewide SOICCs can receive a directory of state-based systems from the Association of Computer-Based Systems for Career Information (1990), or contact their state's education or labor departments for further information.

In 1990, NOICC provided funding to Colorado State University (Colorado Video Review Project, School of Occupational and Educational Studies, Colorado State University, Fort Collins, CO 80523) for the purpose of establishing guidelines for the review and evaluation of career development videos. This undertaking trains professionals in the review and evaluation of videos, provides a document to assist in the selection of videos, and provides guidelines for video producers. Each video receives a score of 1-4 (Poor, Acceptable, Very Good, Excellent) on each of the following criteria:

Instructional Quality

1. *Content*: Title seems appropriate. Purpose understood early. Content current, accurate. Content load appropriate.
2. *Instructional Design*: Well organized. Presented logically, clearly. Information appropriate for intended audience level. Objectives readily identifiable.
3. *Effectiveness*: Holds interest of intended audience. Stimulates thinking. Creates curiosity. Positively impacts viewer's knowledge, skill, and/or attitude. Motivates response.
4. *Social Orientation*: Role stereotyping (age, sex, race, ethnicity, religion, handicapping condition, etc.) avoided. Value

orientation or social class bias not implied. Appropriate attention to current social issues (e.g., drug and alcohol abuse,
health and wellness, aggression, self-responsibility).
5. *Market Value*: Product is needed. Unique. Timely and useful
shelf life. Appropriate pricing.

Technical Quality

1. *Audio*: Voices, narration are clear, understandable. Sound is
crisp, clean. Background noise minimal. Music, sound effects
appropriate, contribute to message.
2. *Visual*: Focus, color, clarity, exposure are acceptable. Graphics and special effects appropriate, contribute to message.
Attention getting scenes used. Visual impact strong.
3. *Production*: Credits include names, dates, how to obtain information, etc. Camera work is smooth, steady, professional.
Lighting natural, editing smooth.

The first resultant publication, *Colorado Career Development
Reviews*, contains ratings and reviews of 13 videos, and narrative
reviews of an additional 19 videos (Feller & Jacobsen, 1990). More
exhaustive subsequent *Reviews* will be forthcoming.

COMPUTERIZED SYSTEMS AND SOFTWARE
EVALUATIONS

The wide variety of computerized systems (commonly referred
to as computerized information delivery systems—"CIDS," or computer-assisted career guidance systems—"CACG systems") makes
the review and evaluation of such programs particularly challenging. Numerous articles have appeared in the professional literature
outlining criteria for the evaluation and selection of CACG systems
(e.g., Bloch & Kinnison, 1989; Bridges, 1987; Caulum & Lambert,
1985; Forrer, 1987; Harris-Bowlsbey, 1983; Heppner & Johnston,
1985; Maze, 1989; Riesenberg, 1984).

The Winter 1990 edition of the *Journal of Career Development*,
a thematic issue on evaluating CACG systems, contains the most
exhaustive comparative analysis of such systems undertaken to date

(Sampson, Reardon, Humphreys, Peterson, Evans, & Domkowski, 1990). The researchers used a differential cost analysis procedure to compare nine systems (The Career Information System, CHOICES, CHOICES CT, CHOICES Jr., DISCOVER for Colleges and Adults, DISCOVER for High Schools, DISCOVER for Junior High and Middle Schools, Guidance Information System, and SIGI PLUS) in terms of the features available with respect to the costs involved. The "features" represent (a) information for career decision-making/system content, (b) user friendliness/human factors, and (c) support materials and services available from the developer. The "costs" represent (a) system specific costs, and (b) constant costs that exist irrespective of the specific system used. In addition to its value in evaluating and comparing CACG systems, this study assists in the identification of the large number (i.e., 424) of features that can be taken into consideration when examining CACG systems.

In an attempt to assist consumers and producers alike, the NCDA has produced *Career Software Review Guidelines* (NCDA, 1991c). These guidelines consist of one section devoted to the description of the software and a second section containing criteria for evaluating the program. The *Software Evaluation Criteria*, too lengthy for inclusion herein, consists of sixty-seven items scored on a 5-point scale (Unsatisfactory, Poor, Satisfactory, Good, Outstanding). The items fall under the following categories: Information in the Program, Career Development Process, User Interaction, Technical Aspects of the Software and Materials, and Support. The NCDA has also published the *The Counseling Software Guide* (Walz, Bleuer, & Maze, 1989) which contains half-page descriptions of over 150 CACG systems as well as thirty-eight brief program reviews.

ADDITIONAL CRITERION

The aforementioned publications and guidelines may be of use to the librarian contemplating the purchase of particular sources of occupational information. Once its use is instituted, occupational information should be subject to on-going evaluation. Perhaps the most obvious criterion of usefulness of occupational information is the age of the material. Because outdated information may be more harmful than no information at all, periodic weeding or "book burning" (Hoppock, 1976) is strongly recommended. When funding is available, dated material should be replaced, and information on burgeoning careers purchased anew. Given the reality of budgetary constraints, however, one may heed Hoppock's (1976) advice by labelling material more than five years old as follows: "OUT OF DATE: This document is more than five years old. Some of the information in it may now be out of date. Ask your counselor where to get more recent information" (p. 47).

The occupational information's publication date, however, should not be the sole criterion of its worth. A second obvious measure of usefulness is degree of usage. The task of determining the rate of usage is relatively simple with CACG systems that require user sign-ups or log-ons, and which contain internal features for compiling numbers and patterns of usage. With printed materials that may not be checked out, one may follow Biggs's (1990) recommendations for measuring reference collection use by employing such methods as (a) reshelving techniques (i.e., staffers recording items when putting them away), (b) unobtrusive observation of use, (c) user tallies, and (d) exit interviews. An additional unfortunate but inevitable means of determining popularity is the prevalence of theft or "ripped out" articles.

Staff persons should attempt to ascertain if nonuse is a function of the material's quality and appropriateness, or a peripheral factor such as physical inaccessibility, incorrect cataloging, or staff persons' failure to promote its use. Relatedly, heavy usage does not necessarily reflect high quality. This author is aware of one series of career books that receives disproportionately heavy usage due to its attractive packaging and compelling titling rather than to the quality of its content.

This speaks to the need to supplement the aforementioned quantitative evaluations with more qualitative procedures. The simplest and most revealing means of evaluating the worth of occupational information is user satisfaction. The most modest measure can be derived through the use of a librarian-made survey requiring patrons to rate the "quality," "usefulness" or "helpfulness" of a particular resource on a simple Likert-style scale. More ambitious surveys can contain ratings on any number of items gleaned from the aforementioned printed, audiovisual, and computerized career material evaluation guidelines. Exit interviews can serve the same purpose, and supply additional anecdotal information regarding the patrons' reactions and subsequent needs.

CONCLUSION

As the availability and sophistication of occupational information increases, so increases the responsibility of the librarian to select, maintain, and update appropriate and high quality material. By using the resources and guidelines discussed herein, librarians are in a position to facilitate the patrons' career exploration, and, thus, play a crucial role in the career development process.

REFERENCES

American Library Association (1985). *Job and career information centers*. Chicago, IL: ALA.

Association of Computer-Based Systems for Career Information (1990). *1989-90 Directory of state-based career information delivery systems*. Eugene, OR: ACSCI Clearinghouse.

Biggs, M. (1990). Discovering how information seekers seek: Methods of measuring reference collection use. *The Reference Librarian*, No. 29, 103-117.

Bloch, D. P., & Kinnison, J. F. (1989). A method for rating computer-based career information delivery systems. *Measurement and Evaluation in Counseling and Development*, 21, 177-187.

Bridges, M. (1987). Resources to find and evaluate counseling software. *Career Planning and Adult Development Journal*, 3 (2), 34-42.

Brown, S.T. & Brown, D. (1990). *Designing and implementing a career information center*. Garrett Park, MD: Garrett Park Press.

Caulum, D., & Lambert, R. (Eds.) (1985). *Guidelines for the use of computer-based career information and guidance systems*. Eugene, OR: Association of Computer-Based Systems for Career Information, ACSCI Clearinghouse, University of Oregon.

Clack, D.H. (1979). Organizing materials in career counseling information centers. *Library Resources and Technical Services*, 23, 123-128.

Education Information Center Project (1989). *Annotated bibliography of the "best of the best" career books*. Chicago, IL: American Library Association and Public Library Association.

Feller, R. & Jacobsen, B. (May, 1990). *Colorado career development video reviews.* Ft. Collins, CO: School of Occupational and Educational Studies, Colorado State University.

Flanders, R. (1988). The evolution of the NOICC-SOICC programs: 1977-1987. *Journal of Career Development,* 14 (3), 145-159.

Forrer, S. E. (1987). Evaluating career development software. *Career Planning and Adult Development Journal,* 3 (2), 31-33.

Green, C.H. (1979). Managing career information: A librarian's perspective. *Vocational Guidance Quarterly,* 28, 83-91.

Harris-Bowlsbey, J. (1983). The computer and the decider. *The Counseling Psychologist,* 11, 9-14.

Heppner, M. J., & Johnston, J. A. (1985). Computerized career guidance and information systems: Guidelines for selection. *Journal of College Student Personnel,* 26, 156-163.

Hoppock, R. (1976). *Occupational information: Where to get it and how to use it in career education, career counseling, and career development.* New York: McGraw-Hill.

Isaacson, L.E. (1986). Career information in counseling and development. Boston: Allyn & Bacon.

Kirk, B.A., & Michaels, M.E. (1964). *Occupational information in counseling: Use and classification.* Palo Alto, CA: Consulting Psychologist's Press.

Lary, M.S. (1985). Career resource centers. *Library Trends Journal,* 33 (4), 501-512.

Maze, M. (1989). How to evaluate and select software. In G.R. Walz, J.C. Bleuer, & M. Maze (Eds.), *Counseling software guide: A resource for the guidance and human development professions* (pp. 5-7). Alexandria, VA: American Association of Counseling and Development.

Minor, C.W. (1984). Developing a career resource center. In H.D. Burck & R.R. Reardon (Eds.), *Career development interventions* (pp. 169-190). Springfield, IL: Charles C Thomas Publisher.

National Career Development Association (1991a). *Career information print materials review guidelines.* Alexandria, VA: American Association of Counseling and Development.

National Career Development Association (1991b). *Guidelines for the preparation and evaluation of video career media.* Alexandria, VA: American Association of Counseling and Development.

National Career Development Association (1991c). *Career software review guidelines.* Alexandria, VA: American Association of Counseling and Development.

National Diffusion Network (1991). *Educational programs that work.* Longmont, CO: Sopris West.

Public Library Association (1989). *The W.K. Kellogg Foundation Project* (Internal Document No. 39286). Chicago, IL: Author.

Riesenberg, B. (1984). Considerations in the selection of a computerized guidance system. In C.S. Johnson (Ed.), *Microcomputers and the school counselor* (pp. 17-29). Alexandria, VA: American School Counselor Association.

Sampson, J.P., Reardon, R.C., Humphreys, J.K., Peterson, G.W., Evans, M.A., & Domkowski, D. (1990). *Journal of Career Development*, 17 (2), 81-111.

Walz, G., Bleuer, J.C., & Maze, M. (Eds.) (1989). *Counseling software guide: A resource for the guidance and human development professions.* Alexandria, VA: American Association of Counseling and Development.

Zunker, V.G. (1990). *Career counseling: Applied concepts of life planning.* Pacific Grove, CA: Brooks/Cole.

Finding the Right Place to Live: Sources of Geographic Relocation Information

Robert F. Rose

SUMMARY. People move for reasons as varied as economic necessity or the desire to improve their quality of life. Research has shown that moving can be an extremely stressful life event. Libraries can reduce the stress of relocation by providing to those moving information about the area to which they are relocating. Sources and information seeking strategies appropriate to gathering information related to the history, geography, demography, cost of living, climate, educational system, and the cultural, religious, and political environments of different areas, especially smaller cities and towns, are discussed.

INTRODUCTION

People move to new locations for different reasons. Some move out of economic necessity; they may have lost jobs or suffered from plant closings. Others move to improve their quality of life. Some move to advance their careers. Some move because their employer has transferred them or because their company has relocated its business operations. College graduates move to the site of their first post-college position if they do not find (or want) employment in the area where they attended school. Still others move simply to experience life in another part of the country.

Robert F. Rose is Assistant Director for Informational and Instructional Services, Donald O. Rod Library, University of Northern Iowa, Cedar Falls, IA 50613-3675.

Moving, for whatever reason, can be a stressful–and sometimes even traumatic–experience. Moves can be extremely costly, even when subsidized by an employer. Social lives can be disrupted. Those moving may suffer from a lack of a sense of belonging and may have difficulty developing close personal friendships. Families can be separated, particularly those with teenage or college age children. Those moving–particularly those forced to move–may feel a loss of control over their own destiny.[1] They may experience feelings of anxiety, loss, pain, anger and isolation.[2]

Companies transferring employees have traditionally provided assistance in the relocation process. That assistance has been primarily financial. Increasingly, however, companies are considering the human cost of relocation. They have begun to be more involved in such activities as setting up spousal assistance programs, matching transferees with appropriate school systems, considering individual health care issues, and with informing prospective transferees about cultural opportunities in their new location.[3] Compaq and United Van Lines, for example, have developed relatively comprehensive relocation programs.[4]

To ease the stress of relocation, Anderson and Stark propose a five point strategy to alleviate some of its associated problems. That strategy includes: affiliation–developing a commonality of identity and sources of support; preparation and orientation–including comprehensive information about the new location; special assistance for special needs; public relations–to improve the receptivity of relocated families; and research–to survey the needs, gains, satisfactions, and dissatisfactions of transferees.[5]

If relocation is difficult for those being transferred by their employer, the situation for those moving for other reasons is even more difficult and stressful. Libraries can play an important role in alleviating the stresses associated with the relocation process by assisting in the preparation and orientation phase identified by Anderson and Stark.[6]

LIBRARIES AND RELOCATION INFORMATION

Libraries, both public and academic, typically contain a wealth of information that can be of assistance to those contemplating relocation. That information is often in sources not usually thought of in that regard. The primary purpose of this paper is to identify those and other sources of information, and information seeking strategies, that may be helpful in gaining information about specific locales.

Information about larger cities and metropolitan areas is abundant. Although this paper will discuss some of the works that provide information on larger areas, its focus will be on sources that provide information about smaller cities and towns. Sources providing descriptive, rating or ranking, demographic, economic, cost of living, political, cultural and religious, climatological, and education information are included. The paper does not discuss in detail sources that may lead patrons to prospective employers.

Just as reasons for moving vary, so do the needs and interests of patrons seeking relocation information. Some patrons may be interested primarily in relocating to areas that offer enhanced economic opportunities. Some may be more interested in areas that promise a low cost of living. For others, cultural opportunities or other factors may be prime considerations. Some may be looking for the total quality of life "package" offered by an area.

The sources listed in this paper will help provide information about the individual concerns outlined above. Using a variety of these sources will enable the user to develop a relatively comprehensive picture of an area prior to relocating there, thus lessening the possibility of negative surprises and decreasing the stress associated with such moves.

BACKGROUND INFORMATION

Descriptive Information

> Barlow, Diane and Steven Wasserman, eds. *Moving and Relocation Sourcebook.* Detroit, MI: Gale Research, 1991 (scheduleded).

> *Cities of the United States.* Detroit, MI: Gale Research, 1988-.

> *Encyclopedia of Geographic Information Sources.* Detroit, MI: Gale Research, 1987.

Kane, Joseph Nathan, Steven Anzovin, and Janet Podel, eds. *Facts About the States*. New York: H.W. Wilson, 1989.

World Chamber of Commerce Directory. Loveland, CO: World Chamber of Commerce Directory, 1989-. Annual.

Numerous sources exist which provide either descriptive or background information, or which list sources of information, for geographic areas. Most of these sources concentrate on larger cities or states. Such information can still be quite valuable to those trying to learn about smaller areas. Generally, however, those seeking data on smaller areas must pull together information from a variety of sources.

Encyclopedias can be a good source to start gathering information about cities or areas. General encyclopedias will provide at least some information on many relatively small cities. Gale has recently published *Cities of the United States*, a four-volume encyclopedic treatment of more than 100 urban areas, including at least one from each state. It profiles a city's population, economy, history, recreational facilities, geography and climate, education, communications, and health care. This is a nice effort to compile information but some statistics and information included are already outdated.

Facts About the States provides much standard information (state nickname, seal, flower, etc.) as well as brief information on the state's geography and climate, national sites, culture, education, and a historical chronology. For those considering relocation, its most valuable feature may be its bibliographies which list "Guides to Resources," "[the state] in Literature," and "Selected Nonfiction Sources." The latter two categories are especially helpful to those seeking not only a comprehensive overview of a particular state but also a sense or flavor of its history and culture.

Both the *World Chamber of Commerce Directory* and the *Encyclopedia of Geographic Information Sources* provide lists of sources to which one can refer for additional information. Provided they have enough time, relocation information seekers should always contact local chambers of commerce. If they do not have time to do so, they should at least consult vertical files in local libraries to see if such information is available there. The *Encyclopedia of Geo-*

graphic Information Sources lists directories, guidebooks, periodicals, demographic studies, and economic planning documents for 333 cities, all states, and five geographic regions, but is not nearly as comprehensive as it would appear to be from its title.

Guidebooks of various kinds can provide a surprising amount of useful information, especially for smaller cities. The American Guide Series written and published under the auspices of the Writers Program of the Work Projects Administration during the depression remains one of the best such series. Published in the late thirties and early forties, the series provides a good history of individual states–to that time–as well as geographic information. In fact, the series is still one of the best sources for an overview of a state's topography, geology, flora and fauna. Also provided is detailed descriptive information about larger towns and cities as well as suggested driving "tours" which guide readers through different areas of a state. Those tours also provide information on smaller towns and, very importantly, help to provide a geographical context for a particular area. For city information, these guides are obviously most useful for those parts of the country which have not experienced significant growth since the series was published. For general historical and geographical information, however, they are still useful for all states except, obviously, Alaska and Hawaii.

Other travel guides can also be helpful for gleaning information about an area, especially information related to its cultural and recreational opportunities. These would include the guidebooks published by the American Automobile Association and the Mobil Travel Guide series. For the largest cities, of course, individual travel guides may exist.

Rating and Ranking Sources

Boyer, Rick and David Savageau. *Places Rated Almanac.* New York: Prentice Hall Travel, 1989.

Marlin, John and James S. Avery. *Book of American City Rankings.* New York: Facts on File, 1983.

Thomas, G. Scott. *Rating Guide to Life in America's Small Cities.* Buffalo, NY: Prometheus Books, 1990.

Savageau, David. *Retirement Places Rated.* updated ed. New York: Prentice Hall, 1990.

Americans love to rank things, be they sports teams, universities, or cities. Ranking or rating sources can be extremely useful in gathering information about particular geographic areas, especially for the comparative information they provide. They enable relocation information seekers to compare the area where they might relocate to ones with which they are already familiar. Although rating sources usually focus on larger metropolitan areas, they can be useful to those seeking information on smaller cities as well. Users are sometimes able to extrapolate data from such sources and apply it to proximate areas.

The sources listed above share many elements, but each has certain distinctive features. Marlin's book is now out of date, but may still be of some value. It concentrates on the 100 largest cities in the U.S., presenting considerable data on quality of life indicators, such as environment, population, religion, housing, health (police, fire, and sanitation), and culture and recreation. It also provides brief summaries of each city included.

The *Places Rated Almanac* has largely set the standard for such sources since its initial publication. It rates and ranks 333 metropolitan areas for such factors as cost of living, job outlook, crime, health, transportation, education, the arts, recreation and climate. An excellent source, the *Places Rated Almanac* suffers only, as do all such works, from rapid changes in certain categories–from economic conditions to the number and type of professional sports available in smaller areas. An interesting and valuable feature of this source is a "Preference Inventory" which attempts to help users determine which of the rated factors are most important to them personally in selecting an area in which to live. *Retirement Places Rated* has simply taken the idea of the *Places Rated Almanac* and applied it to a specific situation. Because it is geared towards determining the best locations in which to retire, the rankings vary significantly in most cases from the *Places Rated Almanac*.

The newest rating book is the *Rating Guide to Life in America's Small Cities*. It provides information on much smaller geographic units than do most other sources. It includes data on areas where the central city has at least 15,000 residents and its county at least

40,000. It uses fifty statistical categories to rate areas, within 10 groupings: climate/environment, diversions (recreation, shopping, etc.), economics, education, sophistication (college educated population, population influx, broadcast outlets, etc.), health care, housing, public safety, transportation, and urban proximity. It provides summary information on each "micropolitan" area as well as ranking all 219 areas by their composite scores. This is an excellent source, providing much information not readily available prior to its publication.

Users of such rating or ranking sources must be aware that rankings taken out of context mean very little. What is most important to one individual may be of little importance to another. Further, population size tends to skew ratings. Larger metropolitan areas traditionally do better than smaller ones because their size allows them to support more hospitals, communication outlets, a broader range of cultural activities, and other endeavors than smaller areas can. Comparing an area of 100,000 population to one of a million can be misleading. Each person contemplating relocation must determine those factors most important to him or her and attempt to find an area that reflects those personal preferences.

Demographic and Related Information

> *Editor and Publisher Market Guide.* New York: Editor & Publisher Co., 1924-. Annual.

> Marketing Economics Institute. *MEI Marketing Economics Guide.* New York: MEI, 1973. Irregular.

> *Survey of Buying Power Data Service.* New York: S&MM Magazine, Sales & Marketing Management, 1987-. Looseleaf.

> U.S. Department of Commerce. *County and City Data Book.* Washington, D.C.: Government Printing Office, 1952-. Irregular.

Many standard reference sources provide basic demographic and related data for areas, even smaller geographic units. The *County and City Data Book*, for example, includes statistics on population, crimes, education, electric bills, health, housing, labor force, and local government expenditures, among others. Data is provided for counties and cities of 25,000 or more population and places of 2,500 or more. The exact statistics provided vary according to type of governmental unit–city, county, or state–and are often a few years out of date.

The *Survey of Buying Power Data Service* and the *MEI Marketing Economics Guide* provide similar kinds of information. The first provides data and ranks various metropolitan and other areas in such categories as population, households, and income, and also provides state and regional summaries. The latter presents the "market dimensions" of 1,500 cities, 3,100 counties and all metropolitan areas, again covering such categories as population, households broken out by income groups, retail sales data and the like.

Probably the most useful of the above listed sources is the *MEI Editor & Publisher Market Guide*. In addition to summary statistical sections, it provides information on transportation, population, principal industries, retailing (listing shopping centers, major retail outlets and chain stores) and so on for all U.S. and Canadian cities with daily newspapers. This is a source of special value to those seeking information on smaller cities and towns. Even if a particular town does not have its own daily newspaper, a nearby town is likely to have one and relevant information is thus likely to be found here.

SPECIFIC INFORMATION

Employment Opportunities

> Marlin, John Tepper. *Cities of Opportunity: Finding the Best Place to Work, Live and Prosper in the 1990's and Beyond.* New York: MasterMedia, 1988.

> *Thomas Register of American Manufactures and Thomas Register Catalog File.* New York: Thomas Pub. Co., 1906-. Annual.

> *U.S. Manufacturers Directory.* Omaha, NE: American Business Directories, 1989-. Annual.

A separate article would be necessary to provide a comprehensive list of sources that provide job opportunity information to those seeking to relocate.[7] Nevertheless, several specific works bear mention in light of this paper's focus.

Marlin has identified forty two metropolitan areas as "cities of opportunity"–those cities positioned to grow in the next 10 years. His book is potentially useful for those looking for an area in which they might find increased job opportunities. However, Marlin based his list on the 100 cities with the largest number of non-agricultural jobs so he does not include smaller areas which may also be experiencing significant growth. Although published relatively recently, this work illustrates the speed at which information can become outdated. It lists Boston, Massachusetts and Providence, Rhode Island, as cities of opportunity, both in the New England area experiencing economic problems at the time of this writing.

The directories listed above are but two sources that may provide listings of smaller companies, located in smaller towns and cities. The *U.S. Manufacturers Directory* is particularly useful because of its format. It lists by city, company name, and by SIC those manufacturers with 25 or more employees. It provides standard business directory information. It also includes tables showing the number of industrial concerns by county and by three-digit zip code. State or county industrial or manufacturers directories will also be useful for locating potential employers in smaller towns and cities.

Cost of Living

> American Chamber of Commerce Researchers Association. *Cost of Living Index*. Louisville, KY: ACCRA, 1988-. Quarterly.

> *State Tax Review*. Chicago: Commerce Clearing House. 1941-. Frequency varies.

> *All States Tax Handbook*. Englewood Cliffs, NJ: Prentice-Hall, 1977. Annual.

Cost of living information is not usually provided by the federal government for smaller cities, although some state governments may do so. The *Cost of Living Index* is an invaluable source for such information. It provides detailed data for all areas in which the local chamber of commerce has agreed to participate and includes specific price data for 59 individual items, from chicken to bananas to monthly rent to gasoline to pizza to wine. This is the only source which provides direct comparative information for specific items. It also includes a composite index, measuring relative price levels for all participating places. It does *not* measure inflation.

People relocating frequently overlook the role taxation may play in the cost of living equation. However, tax structures vary enormously from state to state and may have an impact on the decision to move. All things considered, a $25,000 income in a state with a low, or even no, state income tax is worth more than the same income in a state with a very progressive income tax. The sources listed above will provide basic information on taxation in the various states although neither one is exhaustive. The *All States Tax Handbook* is possibly the easier to use in doing a state by state comparison because of its graphic format. Both sources provide basic information on sales, income and other taxes. They include *no* information on local taxes–such as property, wage or income, or sales taxes–or on such things as sales tax exclusions. More localized information is sometimes available from chambers of commerce. For the most detailed information on state tax structures, those seeking to relocate should consult the multi-volume state tax sets published by both the Commerce Clearing House (CCH) and Prentice Hall.

Political Environment

> Barone, Michael. *Almanac of American Politics.* Washington, D.C.: National Journal, 1972-. Biennial.

For many people relocating, the question of the local political environment is largely irrelevant. For others–especially those who have taken a more politically active stance–it may be an important factor. Regardless of the category into which individuals fall, the *Almanac of American Politics* can be an extremely useful source. Not only does it provide specific information on current office holders (governors and federal legislators), but it provides fascinating background information on individual states and their congressional districts. Perhaps most importantly, it tracks changes or trends to give a good picture of how the states or districts have evolved over time. Few sources provide a better "feel" for the people and events which have made a state what it is today. This is a fairly non-conventional source for relocation information, but is highly recommended nonetheless.

Cultural and Religious Life

> *American Art Directory*. New York: Bowker, 1952-. Annual.

> *Art in America: Annual Guide to Galleries, Museums, Artists.* New York: Art in America. 1982-. Annual.

> *Musical America: International Directory of the Performing Arts*. Great Barrington, MA: ABC Leisure Magazines, 1974-. Annual.

> *Official Museum Directory*. Washington, D.C.: American Association of Museums, 1971-. Annual.

> Quinn, Bernard et al. *Churches and Church Membership in the United States 1980: An Enumeration by Region, State and County Based on Data Reported by 111 Church Bodies*. Atlanta, GA: Glenmary Research Center, 1982.

> *Yearbook of American and Canadian Churches*. Nashville, TN: Abingdon Press, 1973-. Annual.

For those who have never lived in smaller cities or towns, the availability of cultural activities may be a serious concern. Fortunately, there are a number of sources available which provide information on cultural events, although there is no single source which lists everything.

The *Official Museum Directory* provides information on more than 6,800 museums across the country, and includes descriptions of their collections, facilities, activities, and hours. It does not, however, list some smaller, privately administered museums. The information provided by the *American Art Directory* is similar to that of the *Official Museum Directory*, but includes library and association galleries as well as museums. *Art in America* includes private and university museums and galleries, as well as public ones. Using all three sources will provide a fairly comprehensive listing of museums and galleries. They will not generally provide information on commercial enterprises that also offer art exhibits.

Possibly the best source for information on performing arts offerings in a particular area is *Musical America*, which lists orchestras, opera companies, choral groups, dance companies and performing arts series. The information is presented on a state by state basis. Although fairly comprehensive, this is not an exhaustive listing, particularly for smaller cities. Again, more detailed information may be available from a local chamber of commerce.

Those who have not lived previously in a less populated area may not realize that much of a smaller community's or area's cultural life may be centered around its colleges and universities. For that reason, the catalogs of those institutions should be consulted. Descriptions of facilities, musical groups, and performing arts or lecture series are usually provided there. Although smaller cities and towns may not offer the breadth and depth of a New York or Chicago, they often offer a surprising variety of cultural events.

Religion is another area of great importance to many people. If individuals are very active in a particular church, they would probably prefer to continue that activity in their new location. Very recent figures for churches and church membership are difficult to find, but *Churches and Church Membership in the United States* does provide that information for 1980, broken out by region, state and county. It includes all religious affiliations. More recent information might be available from chambers of commerce or by writing to a particular denomination's headquarters, whose address can be found in the *Yearbook of American and Canadian Churches*.

Education

Bainbridge, William L. and Steven M. Sundre. *SchoolMatch Guide to Public Schools*. New York: Arco, 1990.

U.S. Department of Education. National Center for Education Statistics. *Digest of Education Statistics*. Washington, D.C.: GPO, 1976-. Annual.

Rankings of the States. Washington, D.C.: 1973-. Annual.

For parents considering relocation, the availability of good school systems in the new area may be a key factor in the decision process. What parents consider a "good" school system may vary considerably. For some, it may be related to such items as the student teacher ratio or awards won by a school. For others, it may be the overall size of the school district, the availability of special programs, or average test scores. During the relocation decision process, parents should attempt to define for themselves those characteristics they seek in a school system.[8]

Traditionally, it has been difficult to track down specific information on all but the country's largest school districts without personally visiting the school district in question. Even then, some information may not always have been available. Sources such as the *Digest of Education Statistics* and *Rankings of the States* have been useful for providing data on a statewide level. The *Digest of Education Statistics*, for instance, includes information about teachers, teacher attitudes, salaries, class size, and expenditures for education, but provides only some information on specific school districts with more than 20,000 students. *Rankings of the States* includes no information at the district level, but does provide data on population, enrollment, attendance, faculty, financial resources, revenues, and expenditures for states.

A new source, the *SchoolMatch Guide to Public Schools*, does provide a fair amount of detail on many, but certainly not all, school systems. In addition to a state-by-state comparison of educational resources, it profiles some 1,200 systems in sixty-six metropolitan areas. Data such as school system size indicators and how the school system compares to others on a national percentile rating scale are included. The percentile ratings cover student teacher ratios, building size, performance on scholarship exams, instructional expenses per pupil and income level of residents. School system administrators are also given the opportunity to comment on their system.

Information can be obtained on the remaining approximately 15,000 public school systems and about 8,000 U.S. accredited private and international schools from the creators of SchoolMatch, but not without cost. For about $100, parents can request a report on school systems within a particular geographic area which "match the [parents'] wants and needs." Information is provided on school systems' academic rigor, finance, school size indicators, and community variables. Further information about this service is available in the *SchoolMatch Guide to Public Schools* described above. The *SchoolMatch* database is also available on compact disc through OCLC's Search CD450 series.

Once again, as with so many other categories, some information on local school districts will probably be available from local chambers of commerce. Some state education departments may also be sources to contact. Provided those relocating have time, they may also want to enter a short-term subscription to a local newspaper. While newspapers may not present such information systematically, they can often provide a sense of the school system–and how it is perceived by the community–not available from other sources.

Climate

Climates of the States. Detroit, MI: Gale Research, 1978.

Ruffner, James A. and Frank E. Bair, eds. *The Weather Almanac: A Reference Guide to Weather, Climate and Air Quality in the United States and Its Key Cities.* 5th ed. Detroit, MI: Gale Research, 1987.

Ruffner, James A. and Frank E. Bair. *Weather of U.S. Cities.* 3rd ed. Detroit, MI: Gale Research, 1987.

Any of the three sources listed above can be useful for obtaining weather information on particular geographic areas. The *Weather of U.S. Cities* presents the weather history for 281 weather stations, including statistics on temperature, humidity, precipitation and wind.

It also includes narrative descriptions of "terrain, water bodies and other topographical features" that influence the weather.

Climates of the States provides a good description of the climatological features of all states. It includes monthly temperature and precipitation norms as well as freeze data for all weather stations within the state. The *Weather Almanac* provides historical weather information for major cities and has articles that discuss various weather topics.

MISCELLANEOUS INFORMATION

Business Dateline. Louisville, KY: UMI/Data Courier, 1985-.

Gale Directory of Publications and Broadcast Media. Detroit, MI: Gale Research, 1990-. Annual.

NewsBank. New Canaan, CT: Newsbank, 1982-.

Magazine Index. Menlo Park, CA: Information Access Co., 1982-.

National Newspaper Index. Menlo Park, CA: Information Access Corp., 1979-.

Besides the sources listed in previous sections, there are a number of others that may be useful for patrons seeking relocation information. Magazine or newspaper articles are among the more obvious.

Several indexes and databases may provide access to relevant information. It is not very likely that information on quite small cities or towns will appear in them, but it is possible. The *Magazine Index* and the *National Newspaper Index* may both be helpful, even though the latter indexes only five major newspapers. The *Business Dateline* database provides full text coverage of a number of regional business publications. Although obviously oriented towards business concerns, such regional publications frequently contain articles of more general interest as well.

Another source to consult for information about different areas is *NewsBank*. *NewsBank* selectively indexes and reproduces on microfiche articles from over 400 newspapers from across the country. It, along with its companion source, *Review of the Arts*, leads users to articles that provide a regional perspective to the news. The one drawback to using *NewsBank* is the difficulty in limiting information to a particular geographic location. For example, an article on housing in a particular city would be listed under the appropriate housing subject category and then provided a geographic breakdown. This is the case even with the CD-ROM index version of the product.

Although local newspapers have been mentioned previously as a source of information, their importance bears repeating. Provided users have the time, they might consider entering a short-term subscription to a newspaper in the area to which they are considering relocating. They might also inquire of the newspaper if it has published special issues or supplements that provide an overview of the area. Along the same lines, other regional or local publications may be helpful in gaining an understanding of the area. Both newspapers and other publications will be listed in the *Gale Directory of Publications and Broadcast Media*.

Yet another source to consult, if obtainable, is the yellow pages section of phone directories. A surprising amount of information is available there, not only in the sections concerning the community itself, but also simply by browsing through categories of interest.

One other potentially useful approach is available to those who subscribe to electronic bulletin board or other computer communication services. It might be worth trying to contact people in the area to which the user might relocate. Such services are increasingly used as job search tools.[9] Their usefulness for gathering geographic information has not yet been fully tested–or at least not yet reported.

CONCLUSION

It is obvious from the foregoing that library patrons seeking geographic relocation information have many sources they can consult, even for areas with small populations. The strategy they follow to find that information will depend on several factors: their specific information needs, the time they have to gather the information before making a decision, and the availability of particular sources in nearby libraries.

No source is an adequate substitute for a personal visit to the area in question. However, even when making such a visit, people are well advised to gather as much information as possible before making the trip in order to make the time they spend there as fruitful as possible. They will have a better idea of what to expect before going, and they will have a better idea of what questions to ask during the visit itself.

One final note. There *will* be instances where a community about which information is sought is so small that highly specific information on it will not be obtainable. In those cases, data will have to be extrapolated from larger communities located nearby.

Users should be able to find sufficient data on which to make a good relocation decision if they follow a logical approach to obtaining information and consult appropriate sources. That "good decision" will decrease the stress associated with moving and should help make life in the new location more successful and happier.

REFERENCES

1. Pinder, Craig C. "The Dark Side of Executive Relocation," *Organizational Dynamics* 17 (Spring 1989): 48-58.

2. Gaylord, Maxine and Estelle Symons. "Relocation Stress: A Definition and a Need for Services," *Employee Assistance Quarterly* 2 (Fall 1986): 31-36. For further information on the problems encountered particularly by those who move frequently, and "mobility syndrome," see Anderson, Charlene and Carolyn Stark. "Psychosocial Problems of Job Relocation: Preventive Roles in Industry," *Social Work* 33 (January-February 1988): 38-41. For a comprehensive overview of research on relocation stress, see Brett, Jeanne M. "The Effect of Job Transfer on Employees and Their Families," in *Current Concerns in Occupational Stress*, edited by C. L. Cooper and R. Payne. New York: John Wiley, 1980.

3. Bramlage, John C. "All the Right Moves: A New Strategy for Successful Relocation," *Personnel* 65 (May 1988): 40-43.

4. Beddome, Elaine. "Compaq's Relo Program Goes the Extra Mile," *Personnel Journal* 68 (June 1990): 88-94, and Fritz, Norma R. "Smoothing the Rocky Road to Relocation," Personnel 66 (November 1989): 27-35.

5. Anderson, Charlene and Carolyn Stark. "Emerging Issues from Job Relocation in the High Tech Field: Implications for Employee Assistance Programs," *Employee Assistance Quarterly* 1 (Winter 1985/86): 37-54.

6. *Ibid.*

7. See Rose, Robert F. "Conducting Research on Potential Employers: Report on Cooperative Workshop," *RQ* 27 (Spring 1988): 404-409, for a partial listing of such sources.

8. For an interesting discussion of school systems and what users seek of them, see: Bainbridge, William L. and Steven M. Sundre. "Grading School Systems To Match Transferee's Needs," *Personnel Journal* 66 (May 1987): 120-122, and "Parents as Consumers of Public Education," *Education Digest* 56 (December 1990): 41-42, by the same authors.

9. Naver, Michael. "The Online Job Search," *CompuServe Magazine* 10 (March 1991): 12-14.

Library Resources on the Employment of People with Disabilities

Samuel T. Huang

SUMMARY. This chapter brings together a number of sources on the employment of individuals with disabilities for both employers and employees. It is designed as a guide to assist disabled individuals, educators, librarians, service professionals, and employers who have made a commitment to assist or employ disabled people to locate needed information dealing with employment.

AMERICANS WITH DISABILITIES ACT, 1990

Employment has been at the top of the list of major concerns for people with disabilities in the United States.[1] The recently-enacted Americans with Disabilities Act of 1990 (ADA) has made a great impact on the employment of the disabled. In general, the new law states that all businesses with the exception of those that employ less than fifteen people, must have facilities that accommodate disabled employees. With this ruling, the library plays a vital role in building a core collection of various subjects relating to the employment of the physically disabled, and making these resources available to assist employers or employees in modifying and interpreting the laws and regulations. The intent of this article is to assist people with disabilities who are looking for employment, as

Samuel T. Huang is an Associate Professor at the University Libraries, Northern Illinois University, DeKalb, IL 60115. Professor Huang was formerly the Libraries' coordinator for visually impaired students.

well as librarians, educators, and other service professionals who work with disabled individuals.

Beginning in 1990, Thompson Publishing Group published an *ADA Compliance Guide* in a looseleaf format combining with it a monthly newsletter.[2] This compliance guide offers an overview and history of the ADA, its applicability, information on accommodations in workplace settings and buildings, enforcement and penalties, and guides to every state's disability laws. The publisher has reserved several sections to cover forthcoming regulations and transportation accessibility. A special report on the ADA of 1990 was published by the Bureau of National Affairs (BNA).[3] This report provides a thorough treatment of the ADA. It includes not only a history of the act, but also contains a section-by-section analysis, legal analysis, compliance, a question-and-answer section, and profiles of employers which have programs in place for employees with disabilities. A text of the act, the conference report, and a directory of agencies and organizations are also included.

There are several other publications relating to the Americans with Disabilities Act of 1990. Several of these are succinct but thorough, such as the *Americans with Disabilities Act of 1990: Laws and Explanation*[4] which is an excellent source for legislative history reference to the *Congressional Record,* and Jackson's *Americans with Disabilities Act: Making the ADA Work for You,*[5] designed as a training manual for employers. The latter covers a wide variety of practical issues such as pre-employment screening, recruitment, interviewing, reasonable accommodation, supervision, integration, and promotion issues. In order to comply with the law, employers should acquire several resources for reference purposes. A compliance manual, *What Business Must Know About the Americans with Disabilities Act,* published by the U. S. Chamber of Commerce,[6] offers valuable information to assist employers in understanding the ADA. To get a quick overview of the ADA, the U. S. Equal Opportunity Commission (EEOC) has produced a twenty-minute video with open-captions entitled, *Expanding Equal Opportunities.*[7] This video not only presents an overview and analysis of the EEOC's role in enforcing the ADA, but also presents some practical guidance for employers.

Another resource is the Job Accommodation Network (JAN) which offers a toll-free telephone consultation.[8] JAN allows the employer to receive brief descriptions of accommodations made in situations similar to the job being considered from human-factor consultants. It will assist if one needs to accommodate an applicant with a disability, a new employee, or an employee who is newly-disabled. Additional resources are available at the state and local level. Employers or employees should contact one's Governor's Committee on Employment of People with Disabilities for local resources.

Finally, in response to a Congressional request for data on the potential cost of implementing the Americans with Disabilities Act, particularly in the private sector, the United States General Accounting Office publishes a book entitled, *Persons with Disabilities.*[9]

SOURCES FOR SUCCESSFUL EMPLOYMENT

A good attitude toward work is important when an individual is trying to seek a job. Books and audio tapes dealing with this topic are good resources to use as guides in developing the right attitude. *The Assertive Job Seeker*[10] is a three-part audiocassette produced especially for the blind and visually impaired. The cassettes contain sections on assertiveness, general job seeking methods, supportive organizations, and technical aids. The project was sponsored by the President's Committee on Employment of People with Disabilities. Another free sound recording, *A Job in Your Future*,[11] again produced especially for the blind and visually impaired, includes information and practical advice from job hunting experts and visually impaired individuals who found jobs they enjoyed and performed successfully.

There are numerous books which also relate to successful employment. Greenwald's *Be the Person You Were Meant to Be: Antidotes to Toxic Living*[12] suggests ways to live an emotionally rich life, including the risks in seeking employment. Identifying elements of a successful life and applying these elements to entering the job market are well presented in Nash's *Get the Best of Yourself.*[13] Several other books aid disabled and able-bodied individuals alike to build a positive, good attitude toward work, such as Browne's *How I Found Freedom in an Unfree World.*[14] This book provides suggestions about all aspects of life including jobs, such as "starting from zero" in assessing attitudes and plans for future employment. Both Lair's *I Ain't Well–But I Sure am Better*[15] and Kelly's *How to Make Your Life Easier at Work*[16] are in-depth examinations at building better communication and commitment. They urge discovery of "positives" in the work setting and keeping the job in proper perspective.

A revised and enlarged edition of Ziglar's *See You at the Top*[17] is a "how to" book that aims to do away with "stinkin' thinkin'" and "hardening of the attitudes." Ziglar's work explores self-image, relations with others, attitudes, goals, desires, and work. In Bolles' *The Three Boxes of Life: and How to Get Out of Them,*[18] finding meaning in one's work and measuring one's effectiveness are discussed in the context of learning, achieving, and playing during each stage of life. Bolles' *What Color is Your Parachute?,*[19] which first appeared in 1972 and is now updated annually, details procedures for life planning, choosing a career, and job seeking. It contains sections on help available to the job seeker, rejection, what to do and where to do it, and the importance of identifying the person who can hire you and presenting him/her with your skill. It also includes a section, "Help with Special Problems of Handicapped Job Hunters."

The President's Committee on Employment of People with Disabilities has published many helpful books and pamphlets.[20] For example, *Job Tips for People with Mental or Emotional Problems*[21] offers advice for the mentally restored on job hunting, legal rights and how to act on the job. It includes information on mental illness and its influence on work and community resources. The President's Committee has also published *Planning for a Job: Tips for Disabled Students*[22] which contains many suggestions for "work readiness" and vocational skills. Both of these publications are free to interested individuals. A small booklet published by the Committee, *Ready, Willing, and Available: A Business Guide for Hiring*

People with Disabilities[23] has been prepared by volunteer representatives from companies with long records of hiring people with physical, mental or learning disabilities. It can be used as a guide for companies or institutions that have made commitments to employ disabled persons.

In 1982, the Greater Detroit Society for the Blind produced a braille edition of *Tips and Topics for the Visually Impaired Job Seeker.*[24] This publication in special format answers many job seekers questions and suggests many interviewing skills. These techniques are especially important to the visually impaired and blind job seeker.

For those companies or institutions wanting to make a real commitment to employing the disabled person, Rabby's *Locating, Recruiting and Hiring the Disabled*[25] proves to be a valuable reference source. The book opens with an assessment of the disabled labor pool. Rabby describes strategies which personnel managers can employ to locate or develop qualified applicants among the disabled. His emphasis is on innovative approaches that reach beyond the traditional rehabilitation system. This book consists of six appendices which list publications, agencies, organizations, and private firms that are concerned with the disabled. These lists are useful for recruiters to obtain access to the disabled or to learn more about disabled individuals' needs.

Libraries and librarians have produced several sources on the topic of employment of disabled persons. The United States Equal Employment Opportunities Commission Library published a bibliography entitled, *Library Resources on the Employment of Individuals with Disabilities.*[26] Though it contains selective, annotated materials (both books and periodical articles) located in the U. S. Equal Employment Opportunities Commission Library, it can be used as a basic guide to assist disabled persons in locating needed information on the subject of employment. *The World of Work: The Handicapped Person's Guide to Finding a Job,*[27] is produced by the Association of Specialized and Cooperative Library Agencies (ASCLA), a division of the American Library Association. The book contains many landmark books on career information for people with specific disabilities. Finally, Wright's *Library Mana-*

ger's Guide to Hiring and Serving Disabled Persons[28] contains valuable information relating to hiring people with disabilities.

LEGAL RESOURCES

Once disabled individuals are hired, they should be aware of their legal rights and their responsibilities on the job. There are several publications which will assist employers and employees to understand their legal rights. Burgdorf's *Legal Rights of Handicapped Persons*[29] is a standard source. Though it is dated, it is still useful for background material. To update Burgdorf's treatise, Goldman's *Disability Rights Guide*[30] provides explanations of the spectrum of laws affecting individuals with disabilities on employment, housing, education, transportation and more. In addition, every library should own a copy of the *Handicapped Requirements Handbook*.[31] This looseleaf publication with its monthly updates contains essential information and requirements related to Section 504 of the Rehabilitation Act of 1973, as amended, including the related statues. It also includes court case abstracts, a self-evaluation questionnaire, copies of regulations, and a set of the American National Standards Institute (ANSI) standards relating to building accessibility. Another publication, published by the National Council on the Handicapped, entitled *Toward Independence*,[32] is a report to the President and the Congress of the United States which provides descriptions of federal legislation and programs affecting people with disabilities. The report also makes an assessment of how well the laws are working and makes suggestions for improvement.

There are three sources which deal with the rights of specific disabilities. The first publication, *Legal Rights of Hearing Impaired*,[33] deals with employment, housing, education, telecommunications, and health care of the hearing impaired. The second source, Parry's *Mental Disability Law: a Primer*,[34] includes definitions of key terms, an overview of federal laws, and an analysis of important cases. Material covered in Parry's book is drawn from the *Mental and Physical Disability Law Reporter*.[35] The final source is Rothstein's *Rights of Physically Handicapped Persons*,[36] a standard treatise covering education, employment, public access, transportation, etc. Of course, laws are constantly changed, updated and implemented. Libraries should be aware of the availability of new resources relating to laws and legislation which affect the people with specific disabilities.

WORKPLACE ACCOMMODATION AND ACCESSIBILITY

In 1988, Gael's *Job Analysis Handbook for Business, Industry, and Government*[37] gathered manuscripts from a multitude of experts. Among the many subjects considered are planning for job analysis, methods for obtaining job information, and job analysis applications for specific occupations, such as clerical jobs and police officers. The U. S. Office of Personnel Management published a comparable work to Gael's handbook, *Handbook of Job Analysis for Reasonable Accommodation*[38] to focus on a job analysis process to plan and select appropriate action to accommodate handicapped individuals in specific jobs in the work environment.

When employers hire disabled people or have employees who become disabled after employment, they should make reasonable accommodation to meet the needs of these individuals. There are many resources toward this end which are useful for employers, librarians, educators, and service professionals. Bowe's *Reasonable Accommodation Handbook*[39] is developed specifically for the American Telephone and Telegraph Company. This looseleaf binder contains photographs and descriptions of the products which can make the workplace accessible to employees with disabilities. Many examples of action that can be taken to accommodate individuals with disabilities in the workplace are covered in the *Handbook on Reasonable Accommodation*[40] and the *Handbook of Job Analysis for Reasonable Accommodation* (previously listed). A total resource for the wheelchair community, Maddox's *Spinal Work*[41] contains a chapter which describes the many types of spinal injuries as well as sections on sports and recreation, travel, disability rights, and using computers.

REFERENCE SOURCES

Another effective method for finding a job, regardless if one is able-bodied or disabled, is to write unsolicited letters and send resumes to employers. The *Directories in Print*[42] will assist applicants in locating directories that will provide addresses of prospective employers. This annotated guide covers over 14,000 directories published worldwide. A similar work of this nature is the *Encyclopedia of Associations*[43] which covers over 30,000 national and international organizations, including trade, business and commercial, agricultural and commodity, legal, governmental, public administration, etc. Another reference guide to assist patrons is the *Encyclopedia of Governmental Advisory Organizations*,[44] plus its supplement, *New Governmental Advisory Organizations*.[45] Both titles serve as a reference guide to more than 5,400 permanent, continuing, and ad hoc U. S. presidential advisory committees, public advisory committees, interagency committees, and other government-related boards.

The Encyclopedia of Careers and Vocational Guidance[46] offers a lot of important information relating to various careers in detail. The appendix in volume four includes a section, "Resources and Associations for Individuals with Disabilities." This section will lead disabled individuals, librarians, and professionals in the field to the related agencies at the state and local levels.

In general, the federal government appropriates funds for programs in states and cities. Each state determines the allocation of the funds and sponsors its own programs. For this reason, it is significant to consult the above mentioned resources for specific information. Most federally-sponsored programs for the disabled are operated through the U. S. Department of Education which focuses on vocational rehabilitation, education, financial and medical assistance, civil rights, housing, tax benefits, and public transportation. The Department can direct a disabled person to any relevant program. The appendix of *The Encyclopedia of Careers and Vocational Guidance* services as a quick reference to government-sponsored agencies and national organizations for people with specific disabilities.

PERIODICALS

In discussing the library resources on the employment of individuals with disabilities, periodical publications are vital resources. Because of new laws and changes in legislation, many publications become obsolete quickly. Many periodical indexes will assist patrons to locate articles related to employment of individuals with disabilities. The basic periodical guide is *Ulrich's International Periodical Directory*[47] for selecting periodicals related to the disability. This annual publication with quarterly updates provides bibliographical information for over 116,000 periodicals. This publication includes works from around the world. The titles are arranged alphabetically under approximately 550 broad subject headings. Periodicals relating to the employment of individuals with disabilities are classified under Deaf, Blind, Education–Special Education and Rehabilitation, Social Services and Welfare. Patrons also can use this guide to find where a certain periodical is indexed. A similar publication to Ulrich's is *The Standard Periodical Directory*[48] which lists, sometimes with brief annotations, thousands of house organs, newsletters, reports, and so on. The fourteenth edition (1991) of the directory lists more than 75,000 magazines, including approximately 5,000 newsletters, 4,000 house organs, 7,000 directories, and 20,000 bulletins, association publications and other types of ephemeral materials. Here, however, the titles listed are limited to those published in the United States and Canada. It is a useful backup for Ulrich's, particularly as it includes types of work not found in the other directory.

For specific results, one should turn to Katz's *Magazines for Libraries*.[49] This select annotated list is revised every three years and lists more than 6,500 periodicals under more than 130 subject headings. The descriptive and critical annotations are by experts in the field. The annotations point out the strengths and weaknesses of each title for different readers. There is a specific section dealing with disabilities in this book, but many related subjects can also be found in the Special Education or Government Periodicals sections. Many if not most libraries purchase these three major selection tools.

In addition to the above three standard periodical sources, several bibliographies dealing with disabilities are helpful in finding periodicals, newsletters, and special looseleaf publications dealing with employment of disabled individuals. Velleman's *Meeting the Needs of People with Disabilities*[50] includes a chapter on books and periodical resources for core collections, useful for all library and information settings. It is presently topical so that collections may be assembled according to one's needs.

SUPPORTED AND COMPETITIVE EMPLOYMENT

There are several books which cover employment, transition, and supported employment in general. To name a few, Bellamy's *Supported Employment*[51] contains sections on program models, strategies for state leadership, parents, advocates and friends, and business participation. Since the late 1960s, a significant change has occurred in the provision of services to persons with severe disabilities. Gardner's *Toward Supported Employment*[52] provides good insight into how the community has responded to the changes based on court ruling and judicial decision-making.

Several works address the issues and practices of competitive employment currently in use or under development regarding the employment of disabled persons. Rusch's *Competitive Employment Issues and Strategies*[53] combines a wealth of information that is either unavailable in published form or scattered across a number of sources, many of which are not readily accessible to practicing professionals. It is a good resource to anyone interested in adult services for individuals with disabilities. Other books such as Kiernan and Stark's *Pathways to Employment for Adults with Developmental Disabilities*,[54] Ianacone and Stodden's *Transition Issues and Directions*,[55] and Wehman's *Vocational Rehabilitation and Supported Employment*[56] also address the topic of competitive employment.

Other materials owned by public, academic and special libraries may be located by checking the subject card catalog or the online catalog. There are many new and forthcoming publications dealing with this subject. Many online databases and CD-ROM databases also can help an individual to locate current articles or books. One should consult with a reference librarian for further information.

REFERENCES

1. National Council on the Handicapped. *On the Threshold of Independence: A Report to the President and the Congress of the United States.* Washington, DC: National Council on the Handicapped, 1988, p. 45.

2. *ADA Compliance Guide.* Washington, DC: Thompson Publishing Group, 1990-. Looseleaf.

3. *Americans with Disabilities Act of 1990: A Practical Guide to Impact, Enforcement, and Compliance.* [BNA Special Report.] Washington, DC: Bureau of National Affairs, 1990.

4. *Americans with Disabilities Act of 1990: Law and Explanation.* [Labor Law Reports, Employment Practices, "Extra Edition," No. 395, July 31, 1990.] Washington, DC: Commerce Clearing House, 1990.

5. Jackson, Lewis, ed. *Americans with Disabilities Act: Making the ADA Work for You.* Washington, DC: Milt Wright & Associates, Inc., 1990.

6. *What Business Must Know About the Americans with Disabilities Act.* Washington, DC: Chamber of Commerce, January 1991.

7. *Expanding Equal Opportunities: Implementing the Americans with Disabilities Act.* Washington, DC: U. S. Equal Employment Opportunities Commission, Office of Communications and Legislative Affairs, 1990.

8. Job Accommodation Network (JAN) toll-free consultation (800-526-7234). Washington, DC: The President's Committee on the Employment of People with Disabilities, 1111 20th St., NW, Suite 636, Washington, DC 20036-3470.

9. United States. General Accounting Office. *Persons with Disabilities: Reports on Costs of Accommodations.* Washington, DC: U. S. General Accounting Office, 1990.

10. Bruck, Lilly. *The Assertive Job Seeker.* New York: In Touch Networks, Inc., 1982.

11. Kimbrough, Louise. *A Job in Your Future.* Berwyn, IL: Dialogue, 1982.

12. Greenwald, Jerry A. *Be the Person You Were Meant to Be: Antidotes to Toxic Living.* New York: Dell Publishing, 1979.

13. Nash, Katherine. *Get the Best of Yourself: How to Find Your Success Pattern and Make It Work for You.* New York: Grossett and Dunlap, 1976.

14. Browne, Harry. *How I Found Freedom in an Unfree World.* New York: Avon, 1974.

15. Lair, Jess. *I Ain't Well–But I Sure am Better.* New York: Fawcett Crest, 1976.

16. Kelly, Al. *How to Make Your Life Easier at Work*, 2nd ed. New York: Avon, 1990.

17. Ziglar, Zig. *See You at the Top*, rev. and enlarged ed. Gretna, LA: Pelican, 1987.

18. Bolles, Richard Nelson. *The Three Boxes of Life: And How to Get Out of Them.* Berkeley, CA: Ten Speed Press, 1981.

19. _____, *What Color Is Your Parachute? A Practical Manual for Job Hunters and Career Changers.* Berkeley, CA: Ten Speed Press, 1991.

20. The President's Committee on Employment of People with Disabilities (Formerly: The President's Committee on Employment of the Handicapped), 111 20th St., NW, Suite 636, Washington, DC 20036-3470. (202) 653-5044 (Voice), (202) 653-5050 (TTD), (202) 653-7386 (FAX).

21. *Job Tips for People with Mental or Emotional Problems.* Washington, DC: The President's Committee on Employment of the Handicapped, 1982.

22. *Planning for a Job: Tips for Disabled Students.* Washington, DC: The President's Committee on Employment of the Handicapped, 1982.

23. *Ready, Willing, and Available: A Business Guide for Hiring People with Disabilities*, 3rd ed. Washington, DC: The President's Committee on Employment of People with Disabilities, February 1991.

24. Pumo, Benjamin J. *Tips and Topics for the Visually Impaired Job Seeker.* Detroit, MI: Detroit Society for the Blind, 1982.

25. Rabby, Rami. *Locating, Recruiting and Hiring the Disabled.* New York: Pilot Books, 1981.

26. *Library Resources on the Employment of Individuals with Disabilities.* Washington, DC: U. S. Equal Employment Opportunities Commission Library, November 1990.

27. Minor, Dorothy, comp. *The World of Work: The Handicapped Person's Guide to Finding a Job* (ASCLA Occasional Paper #2). Chicago, IL: Association of Specialized and Cooperative Library Agencies, American Library Association, 1984.

28. Wright, Keith C. and Judith F. Davie. *Library Manager's Guide to Hiring and Serving Disabled Persons.* Jefferson, NC: McFarland, 1990.

29. Burgdorf, Robert L., Jr., ed. *Legal Rights of Handicapped Persons: Cases, Materials, and Text: 1983 Supplement.* Baltimore, MD: Paul H. Brookes, 1983.

30. Goldman, Charles. *Disability Rights Guide: Practical Solutions to Problems Affecting People with Disabilities*, 2nd ed. Lincoln, NB: Media Pub., 1991.

31. *Handicapped Requirements Handbook*, 2 vols. Washington, DC: Federal Programs Advisory Service, 1983-.

32. National Council on Handicapped. *Toward Independence: An Assessment of Federal Laws and Programs Affecting Recommendations....*Washington, DC: Government Printing Office, 1986.

33. National Center for Law and the Deaf. *Legal Rights of Hearing Impaired People*, 3rd ed. Washington, DC: Gallaudet College Press, 1986.

34. Parry, John, ed. *Mental Disability Law: A Primer*, 3rd ed. Washington, DC: American Bar Association, Commission on the Mentally Disabled, 1984.

35. *Mental and Physical Disability Law Reporter*. Washington, DC: American Bar Association, 1984.

36. Rothstein, Laura F. *Rights of Physically Handicapped Persons*. New York: McGraw-Hill, 1984.

37. Gael, Sidney, ed. *Job Analysis Handbook for Business, Industry and Government*, 2 vols. New York: Wiley, 1988.

38. United States. Office of Personnel Management. *Handbook of Job Analysis for Reasonable Accommodation*. Washington, DC: Government Printing Office, 1984.

39. Bowe, Frank. *Reasonable Accommodation Handbook*. American Telephone and Telegraph, 1983.

40. United States. Office of Personnel Management. *Handbook on Reasonable Accommodation*. Washington, DC: Government Printing Office, 1984.

41. Maddox, Sam. *Spinal Network*, 2nd ed. Boulder, CO: Spinal Network, 1990.

42. Montney, Charles B., ed. *Directories in Print*, 8th ed. Detroit, MI: Gale, 1991.

43. Burek, Deborah M., ed. *Encyclopedia of Associations*, 25th ed. Detroit, MI: Gale, 1991.

44. Allard, Denise M. and Donna Batten, eds. *Encyclopedia of Governmental Advisory Organizations*, 6th ed. Detroit, MI: Gale, 1990.

45. _____, *New Governmental Advisory Organizations*. A supplement to the 6th edition of *Encyclopedia of Governmental Advisory Organizations*. Detroit, MI: Gale, 1991.

46. Hopke, William E., ed. *The Encyclopedia of Careers and Vocational Guidance*, 4 vols., 8th ed. Chicago, IL: J. G. Ferguson, 1990.

47. *Ulrich's International Periodicals Directory*, 3 vols., New York: Bowker, 1991. Annual, quarterly updates.

48. *The Standard Periodical Directory*, 14th ed. New York: Oxbridge, 1991.

49. Katz, Bill, and Linda Sternberg Katz, eds. *Magazines for Libraries*, 6th ed. New York: Bowker, 1989.

50. Velleman, Ruth A. *Meeting the Needs of People with Disabilities: A Guide for Librarians, Educators, and other Service Professionals*. Phoenix, AZ: Oryx, 1990.

51. Bellamy, G. Thomas, Lary E. Rhodes, David H. Mank, and Joyce M. Albin, eds. *Supported Employment: A Community Implementation Guide*. Baltimore, MD: Paul H. Brookes, 1988.

52. Gardner, James F. *Toward Supported Employment: A Process Guide for Planned Changes*. Baltimore, MD: Paul H. Brookes, 1988.

53. Rusch, Frank R., ed. *Competitive Employment Issues and Strategies*. Baltimore, MD: Paul H. Brookes, 1986.

54. Kiern, William E. and Jack A. Stark, eds. *Pathways to Employment for Adults with Developmental Disabilities.* Baltimore, MD: Paul H. Brookes, 1986.

55. Ianacone, Robert N. and Robert A. Stodden, eds. *Transition Issues and Directions.* Reston, VA: Council for Exceptional Children Division on Mental Retardation, 1987.

56. Wehman, Paul and Sherril M. Moon, eds. *Vocational Rehabilitation and Supported Employment.* Baltimore, MD: Paul H. Brookes, 1988.

An Evaluation of the Resume Content Recommendations of Resume Writing Books

Barbara E. Weeg

SUMMARY. Self-help resume writing books can enable resume writers to make informed decisions concerning appropriate resume content. Librarians who endeavor to meet the career information needs of job seekers have a responsibility to maintain the quality of the resume writing books in library collections. This study utilized the resume content preferences of personnel administrators to explore whether a sample of resume writing books made appropriate resume content recommendations for college graduates seeking entry-level positions. Analysis revealed that the resume books recommended including the resume content items that were preferred by the personnel administrators. However, rather than recommending definite exclusion or inclusion of items personnel administrators preferred not to see on resumes, the books tended not to mention these items or made conditional recommendations. The implications of the major research findings are discussed and additional research is recommended.

INTRODUCTION

Resumes play a central role throughout the employee selection process, from initial screening through interviewing and into post-interview candidate evaluation. Job seekers, therefore, need to be able to develop effective resumes that contain appropriate types of information. Many turn to resume writing books to learn how to

Barbara E. Weeg is a Reference Librarian and the Career Collection Bibliographer at the Donald O. Rod Library, University of Northern Iowa, Cedar Falls, IA 50613-3675.

153

prepare resumes. Self-help resume writing books instruct and advise job seekers about the purposes, preferred contents, and desirable formats of resumes. Resume writing books often contain exercise pages or worksheets designed to help job seekers identify their educational achievements, work histories, skills, and occupational goals. Sample resumes serve to illustrate the application of the instructions given in the resume writing books.

Librarians who endeavor to meet the career information needs of job seekers should strive to provide resume writing books of high quality. However, previous research indicates that the instructions and advice given in resume writing books may not be appropriate. Feild and Holley (1976) compared the resume content recommendations of one frequently used book, the 1972 *College Placement Annual*, to the resume contents preferred by the personnel administrators they surveyed. These researchers determined that several of the items that the *Annual* recommended for inclusion on resumes were considered relatively unimportant by the personnel administrators. Ryland and Rosen (1987) examined popular resume writing books and articles and determined that personnel professionals did not prefer the resume formats in the ways discussed by the resume writing sources.

The purpose of this study is to explore whether current resume writing books provide appropriate instructions to job seekers. Specifically, the major resume content preferences of personnel administrators will be used to evaluate whether a sample of resume writing books makes appropriate resume content recommendations for college graduates seeking entry-level positions. Appropriate resume content items are not established solely by employer preferences. Since there are equal employment opportunity laws designed to protect the rights of job applicants, these laws will be discussed when pertinent.

METHOD

Ten resume books were studied. This represented a 10 percent sample of the number of books listed in the resumes (employment) section of the *Subject Guide to Books in Print* (1990). Efforts were made to insure that high quality, contemporary resume books were chosen for this study. Since a literature review did not identify any lists of recommended resume books, the following selection criteria were used. The books selected needed to focus on resume writing instruction, to have been published recently (1989-1991), to be monographs of at least 80 pages, and to be appropriate for college graduates who seek entry-level positions. Standard selection aids were consulted in identifying resume books for this study. Two books were selected because they had been reviewed in book review journals (Allen, 1990; Eyler, 1990). A list of career titles most in demand by libraries and bookstores from a jobber was identified by searching *Library Journal* ("Career Guides," 1990). The two resume books included on this career best-sellers list were studied (Bostwick, 1990; Jackson, 1990). *Subject Guide to Books in Print* (1990) was used in selecting five other resume books. Books that were listed in *Books in Print* as having been revised or being in second or later editions were chosen since it was assumed that this indicated that the earlier editions had been well-received by resume writers or libraries (Coxford, 1989; Krannich & Banis, 1990; Nadler, 1989; Parker, 1989; Swanson, 1991). One title, the *CPC Annual* (1990), was selected because it is made available in college placement offices nationwide and the resume contents recommended by the 1972 edition had been examined by Feild and Holley (1976).

Each resume book was examined using two rating scales designed by the researcher. The foundation for these rating scales was the resume content preferences of personnel administrators as measured by Harcourt and Krizan (1989). These researchers surveyed 152 personnel administrators in the largest American corporations to determine the resume content items the personnel administrators considered important for new college graduates to include on their resumes, and the items the administrators preferred not to see on resumes or considered unimportant. Other researchers have found that the resume content preferred by employers has changed over the years, partially due to the changing social and legal environment in which employee selection occurs (Olney, 1982; Spinks & Wells, 1987). Therefore, the most recent research concerning resume content preferences was used in developing the scales used in the present study.

The scale of items to include in resumes was constructed by listing the content items considered important by at least 89 percent of the personnel administrators surveyed by Harcourt and Krizan (1989). The resume content items that 78 percent or more of the personnel administrators considered unimportant or rated as items to omit were used in constructing the scale of items not to include in resumes. The researcher read each resume book and evaluated whether the books recommended, did not recommend, sometimes recommended, or did not mention that each content item be included on the resumes of college graduates. The books were evaluated twice in random order to help insure the accuracy of the ratings.

ITEMS TO INCLUDE ON RESUMES

Overall, the resume book authors recommended including on resumes the content items that were preferred by personnel administrators (see Table 1). Although the majority of the instructions given in resume books and the preferences of personnel administrators coincided in terms of content items that are important to include on resumes, there were some areas of difference. Resume book authors and personnel administrators differed concerning whether duties (work experience), job objective, college grade point average, and willingness to relocate should always be included on resumes.

Identification and Contact Information

All of the resume books instructed resume writers to include identification and contact information. Resume books recommended that resume writers place their names, telephone numbers, and addresses in a prominent position on their resumes, usually near the top of the resume (e.g., Nadler, 1989; Swanson, 1991).

Educational Items

Many educational items that the surveyed personnel administrators preferred to see on resumes were considered essential by the authors of the resume books examined. All of the resume books instructed college students or graduates to include on their resumes their academic degrees, names of the colleges from which they graduated, and any college achievements they earned (such as awards or honors).

Nine of the resume books instructed college graduates to indicate the dates they graduated from college in the educational section of their resumes. The majority of the authors indicated that the year of graduation was sufficient (e.g., Jackson, 1990; Krannich & Banis, 1990), although Coxford (1989) recommended including the month of graduation as well. Only one resume book author did not recommend including college graduation dates on resumes. Allen (1990) instructed resume writers to mention their educational credentials briefly, without mentioning the dates they received their degrees. Several pages later, in the section on things to avoid when writing resumes, Allen (1990) explained that resume writers should not provide any information that might reveal their age, including dates they received college degrees, since this might invite age discrimination from employers.

There was less agreement among the resume books concerning whether the educational item of college major should be included on resumes. Ninety-nine percent of the personnel administrators surveyed by Harcourt and Krizan (1989) preferred to see applicants' academic majors on their resumes. Although eight of the resume books also considered college major to be an essential item, two of the resume books were rated as only sometimes instructing college graduates to include their majors. These books gave conditions in which college graduates might not want to list their majors. Eyler (1990) instructed college graduates to indicate their majors only if the graduates believed employers would perceive the majors as relevant to the type of position sought. Jackson (1990) counseled college graduates to consider their range of knowledge so that they did not pigeonhole themselves by seeking only positions they perceived as being closely related to their college majors. He provided sample resumes in which college graduates' majors were not indicated.

There was a considerable difference between the preferences of personnel administrators and the recommendations of resume books

Table 1

Items to Include on Resumes

Resume Content Items	Personnel Administrators Ranking Items Important (%)	Resume Book Recommendations (Number)			
		Include	Exclude	Sometimes	Not Mentioned
Name	100.0	10	0	0	0
Telephone Number	100.0	10	0	0	0
Degree	100.0	10	0	0	0
Name of College	100.0	10	0	0	0
Jobs Held (Titles)	100.0	10	0	0	0
Address	99.3	10	0	0	0
Major	99.3	8	0	2	0
Employing Company(s)	99.3	9	0	1	0

Dates of Employment	99.3	10	0	0	0
Date of College Graduation	95.3	9	1	0	0
Duties—Work Experience	94.7	4	0	6	0
Special Aptitudes/Skills	91.9	10	0	0	0
Job Objective	91.7	5	1	4	0
Awards, Honors—College Achievements	91.4	10	0	0	0
College Grade Point Average	90.8	0	0	9	1
Willingness to Relocate	89.4	2	0	2	6
Achievements—Work Experience	89.2	9	0	1	0

Note. The text in column 1 and data in column 2 are from "A Comparison of Résumé Content Preferences of Fortune 500 Personnel Administrators and Business Communication Instructors" by J. Harcourt and A. C. Krizan, 1989, Journal of Business Communication, 26, p. 181.

concerning the inclusion of college grade point averages on resumes. Ninety percent of the personnel administrators surveyed by
Harcourt and Krizan (1989) preferred to see college grade point
averages on resumes. However, no resume book instructed all college graduates to include their college grade point averages. Rather,
nine of the resume books presented college grade point average as
an optional item and recommended to the graduates, through instructions or illustrations, that they include their grade point averages only if they were favorable. Although most of the nine resume
books did not state a specific grade point level below which graduates should not indicate their grade point averages, Coxford (1989)
stated a grade level of 3.5 and Swanson (1991) a level of 3.0 on a
4-point scale. Several resume book authors explained that positive
information should be emphasized on resumes and that if the graduates' college grades were not complimentary they did not need to
include their grade point averages on their resumes (e.g., Nadler,
1989; Swanson, 1991).

Employment Items

Most of the employment or performance items that the surveyed
personnel administrators preferred to see on resumes also were
considered by the authors of resume books as important items to
include on resumes. Personnel administrators wanted to see job
titles, employment dates, and special aptitudes or skills on the resumes of new college graduates (Harcourt & Krizan, 1989). All of
the resume books instructed resume writers to include the job titles
of the relevant jobs they have held, the dates they were employed
in these positions, and their special aptitudes or skills.

Another employment item that personnel administrators wanted
to see on college graduates' resumes, employer name, was regarded
as an important resume item by the resume books. Nine of the
resume books instructed resume writers to include the names of the
companies at which they have been employed. However, Bostwick
(1990) instructed resume writers to omit their present employers'
names if this information needed to be kept confidential.

A major difference between the preferences of personnel administrators and the instructions given in resume books concerned wheth-

er both job duties and work achievements should be included on resumes. Personnel administrators indicated that they want to learn of the work responsibilities and achievements of new college graduates (Harcourt & Krizan, 1989). In contrast, resume books placed greater emphasis on resume writers specifying the highlights of their work achievements, rather than on outlining all their work duties. Nine of the resume books did instruct resume writers to specify their major work achievements. But only four of the resume books instructed resume writers to specify their job duties. This greater emphasis on work achievements over job duties was seen clearly in the resume books that explained the distinction. For example, Allen (1990) explained that accomplishments should be emphasized since what one was supposed to do (duties) was far less important than what one actually did (achievements).

Job Objective

Concerning the desirability of including job objectives on resumes, there was more variability among resume books than among the personnel administrators. Ninety-one percent of the personnel administrators surveyed by Harcourt and Krizan (1989) indicated that they considered a job objective to be an important item for new college graduates to include on their resumes. Five of the resume books instructed all resume writers to include their job or career objectives on their resumes. For example, Krannich and Banis (1990) informed resume writers that the job objective should be the central focus to which all other items in the resume relate, regardless of the resume type (i.e., chronological, functional, or combination). In contrast, four resume books were rated as only sometimes instructing resume writers to include their job or career objective. The reasons given for not including a job objective differed among the resume books. Eyler (1990) and Jackson (1990) each indicated that a job or career objective was necessary on only certain types of resumes (e.g., the focused or targeted resume). Eyler (1990) also stated that job objectives were optional if applicants' employment objectives were apparent from the resumes themselves. Nadler (1989) and Swanson (1991) instructed resume writers to include job objective statements if they had specific career goals and explained that it was better not to include objectives than to include vague, poorly-written objective statements.

Although personnel administrators preferred new college graduates to include job objective statements on their resumes, some resume book authors had a different perspective. The authors explained that including job objectives might limit the versatility of resumes. Several resume book authors cautioned resume writers that if they included job objective statements they might not be able to use their resumes to pursue jobs in more than one occupational area (e.g., Nadler, 1989). For similar reasons one resume book author instructed all resume writers to omit job objectives. Allen (1990) explained that employers might not consider resume writers who have specified particular job objectives for other available positions, including positions that were much better.

Willingness to Relocate

The resume content item of willingness to relocate appeared to be viewed differently by personnel administrators and resume book authors. Almost 90 percent of the personnel administrators regarded a willingness to relocate statement as an important resume item. In contrast, only two of the resume books advised resume writers to indicate their willingness to relocate and two treated a willingness to relocate statement as an optional item. Six of the resume books did not even discuss or illustrate the willingness to relocate as a possible resume content item. Perhaps resume book authors assumed that applicants would apply for jobs only in geographical areas of interest and that to state the willingness to relocate on resumes would be stating the obvious. Apparently personnel administrators preferred to receive explicit assurance from applicants' resumes that the applicants were willing to relocate.

ITEMS NOT TO INCLUDE ON RESUMES

In analyzing the ways these resume books treated content items, personnel administrators recommended omitting from resumes or considered unimportant, several trends emerged (see Table 2). Rather than recommending definite exclusion or inclusion of these content items, the books tended not to mention these items or made conditional recommendations. Of the thirteen items that personnel administrators preferred not to see on resumes, five of the items were not mentioned in the majority of the resume books. Perhaps the resume book authors assumed that if resume items were not mentioned in their books, the resume writers would not include them on their resumes. Or perhaps the authors preferred not to mention items that should be excluded from resumes. When the books did make conditional recommendations, however, the books tended to discuss reasons for including or excluding personal information and nonvocational activities on resumes. It is possible to examine the appropriateness of these reasons in light of relevant employment legislation.

Personal Information

Several resume books informed resume writers that they might wish to include certain personal characteristics on their resumes; namely, religion, race, gender, personal appearance (photograph), and marital status. The resume books informed resume writers, through comments or examples, that there were circumstances in which they might wish to include this personal information. Coxford (1989) illustrated how resume writers might try to use their marital status and family responsibilities to indicate achievement. Eyler (1990) suggested using family responsibilities such as child-rearing to explain periods of unemployment. Bostwick (1990) and Eyler (1990) each informed resume writers that they might wish to indicate their gender if their names were ambiguous or unclear. Bostwick (1990) advised resume writers to include marital status on resumes without justifying the reasons for his preference. These circumstances did not appear to be legitimate reasons for disclosing personal information.

Not only were some resume book authors advising resume writers to consider including personal characteristics on their resumes, some authors were advising writers to try to manipulate the perceptions of potential employers by using their personal characteristics to gain an advantage over other applicants. Specifically, some re-

Table 2

Items Not to Include on Resumes

Resume Content Items	Personnel Administrators Ranking Items Important (%)	Resume Book Recommendations (Number)			
		Include	Exclude	Sometimes	Not Mentioned
Religion	0.0	0	3	6	1
Race	1.3	0	1	5	4
Gender	2.0	0	4	2	4
Transcript of Grades— High School	2.0	0	0	0	10
Photograph	3.3	0	4	2	4
Marital Status	6.7	0	5	5	0

Birthplace	7.9	0	1	8
Height/Weight	11.2	6	2	2
Church Involvement	16.6	0	9	1
Band, Choral Group, etc.— High School	16.8	0	2	8
Athletic Involvement— High School	17.4	0	3	7
Social Organizations— High School	18.8	0	2	8
Birthdate	21.9	6	3	1

Note. The text in column 1 and data in column 2 are from "A Comparison of Résumé Content Preferences of Fortune 500 Personnel Administrators and Business Communication Instructors" by J. Harcourt and A. C. Krizan, 1989, Journal of Business Communication, 26, p. 188.

sume book authors discussed how resume writers could try to use their religion or marital status to their advantage. Bostwick (1990) and Swanson (1991) stated resume writers might want to include their religion if the writers believed they knew a potential employer's religious preference. Likewise, Krannich and Banis (1990) and Swanson (1991) outlined how resume writers could try to use their marital status to create a favorable impression. Krannich and Banis (1990) stated that identifying marital status might be beneficial if the resume writers were single and applying for jobs requiring considerable travel, or married and applying for jobs requiring stability. Of course, some resume book authors and employment counselors might argue that using one's personal characteristics to create a favorable impression is a necessary technique in a highly competitive job market. Other employment counselors would advise against trying to outguess the preferences of employers that are not job-related. Personnel administrators themselves stated that this personal information should not be included on resumes (Harcourt & Krizan, 1989).

Appropriate resume content is not established solely by employer preferences. Numerous federal, state, and local laws and regulations exist which establish and protect the rights of applicants seeking employment (e.g., Age Discrimination in Employment Act of 1967, Americans with Disabilities Act of 1990, Civil Rights Act of 1964, and Rehabilitation Act of 1973). These laws prohibit discrimination in employment on the basis of age, disabilities, race, color, religion, sex, or national origin. Employers may not discriminate against job applicants when recruiting, screening, hiring, or establishing the conditions of employment for new employees. Employers are required to make every effort to insure that all employee selection devices they use, including application forms and interviews, assess characteristics that are related directly to successful performance on the job in question (Uniform Guidelines, 1990). Although resumes are not mentioned specifically in the law, employers are prohibited from using any personal characteristic information revealed by the job applicants in the selection process in a discriminatory manner. Therefore, resume books that advise resume writers to include personal characteristics such as race or marital status on their resumes may be misinforming their readers. Cautious employers who want to avoid any possibility of discriminating against applicants may reject the resumes of applicants who supply such information.

Several resume books explained that religion, personal appearance, or race could be included on resumes if such personal characteristics were bona fide occupational qualifications. Krannich and Banis (1990) stated religion should be included only if it was a bona fide occupational qualification for a position and Eyler (1990) included religion on the sample resume of a minister. Bostwick (1990) and Krannich and Banis (1990) explained that resume writers should include their photographs only if they were seeking jobs in which personal appearance was a relevant selection criterion, such as in modeling or the theater. Krannich and Banis (1990) stated that race could be included on resumes if it was relevant to one's job objective or was a bona fide occupational qualification. Unfortunately, they did not explain when race would be a legitimate occupational qualification and resume writers might misunderstand their statement.

Some of the resume book authors clearly sought to make their readers informed decision-makers concerning the resume content items of personal characteristics. In total, four of the resume books explicitly mentioned equal employment opportunity laws or affirmative action regulations when explaining why personal characteristics might be omitted from resumes (Allen, 1990; Bostwick, 1990; Coxford, 1989; Nadler, 1989). For example, Nadler (1989) stated that personal data such as height, weight, date and place of birth, and marital status should not be included on resumes. He explained that equal employment opportunity regulations require employers to recruit and hire in a nondiscriminatory manner, without regard to race, handicap, religion, color, sex, age, or national origin, and that such information is now considered to have no bearing on a person's ability to do a job.

Although the resume book authors tended to make only conditional recommendations regarding the inclusion or exclusion of personal information on resumes, in two areas their recommendations corresponded closely to employer preferences. It can be seen on Table 2 that six of the resume books recommended that the personal characteristics of height/weight and birthdate be omitted from all resumes while five of the books recommended that marital status be omitted. However, three of these books did not explain the law. Two of the resume books recommended that resume writers exclude these personal characteristics from their resumes since these characteristics were not relevant to job performance (*CPC Annual*, 1990; Parker, 1989). One book mentioned that resume writers did not need to include these personal characteristics since employers could seek this information if it was legal for them to do so (Jackson, 1990). Although Jackson alluded to the law, he did not explain the relevant laws.

Nonvocational Activities

Church involvement and high school extracurricular activities were items that personnel administrators preferred not to see on resumes. In contrast, resume book authors treated such nonvocational activities as items some resume writers might want to include on their resumes. Nine resume books included church involvement as a resume content item that might be appropriate for some resume writers. Eyler (1990) included church involvement only on the sample resume of a minister since it was a bona fide occupational qualification. The eight other resume books informed resume writers that they might want to include church activities they have participated in to show achievement and to indicate that they are well-rounded individuals who are involved in their communities. Nadler (1989) and Parker (1989) each illustrated how individuals without recent paid work experience could include church leadership activities on their resumes to indicate their skills and accomplishments. Because religion might be used in a discriminatory manner, some resume books advised resume writers to omit or de-emphasize any reference to religious affiliation when including church involvement on their resumes (Allen, 1990; *CPC Annual*, 1990; Coxford, 1989). However, personnel administrators believed that any church involvement should be omitted from resumes. Perhaps personnel administrators believed that resume writers who indicated they participated in church were providing religious information.

Most of the resume books did not suggest that participation in high school extracurricular activities such as band or chorus, athletics, or social organizations be included on the resumes of college graduates. However, three of the resume books did indicate that new college graduates might wish to include high school extracurricular activities on their resumes. Nadler (1989) and Swanson (1991) included all of these high school extracurricular activities as items some resume writers might include on their resumes, while Krannich and Banis (1990) indicated that long-standing participation in an athletic activity (cheerleading) was an appropriate item to include. These resume books demonstrated how recent college graduates who did not have professional work experience could use high school activities to indicate job-related skills such as leadership and creativity. But personnel administrators stated that high school extracurricular involvement was not important for new college graduates to include on their resumes (Harcourt & Krizan, 1989). Employers probably prefer college graduates who have participated in collegiate activities. The resume book authors did instruct recent college graduates to include their collegiate achievements and work experience on their resumes. However, the authors indicated that if college graduates believed their college or work records were not strong, they could include their high school achievements.

CONCLUSION

Several recommendations can be made. First, resume book authors are urged to discuss items that should be omitted from resumes so that resume writers do not unknowingly include these items. Second, resume book authors are urged to mention laws, such as equal employment opportunity or affirmative action, so that job seekers can learn about their employment rights. Third, librarians should take care to select resume books that are current since these books reflect contemporary employer preferences and employment laws. To help resume writers become informed decision-makers about their employment futures, librarians should select titles that instruct about the reasons for including or excluding particular items on their resumes.

Finally, researchers previously concluded that the quality of the resume books available was low (Feild & Holley, 1976; Ryland &

Rosen, 1987). It appears that the quality has improved. Several resume books were particularly noteworthy since they consistently recommended resume items for inclusion or exclusion in the ways preferred by personnel administrators (e.g., Allen, 1990; *CPC Annual*, 1990; Jackson, 1990; Nadler, 1989). However, the present study was limited to a sample of resume writing books appropriate for college graduates seeking entry-level positions. The preferences of personnel administrators at the largest American corporations were used to define appropriate resume content. Perhaps these preferences may not represent the views of all employers. It is recommended that additional research investigate the quality of resume writing books using different audiences and personnel administrator preferences.

REFERENCES

Age Discrimination in Employment Act of 1967, 29 U.S.C. §§ 621-634 (1988).

Allen, J. G. (1990). *Jeff Allen's best: The resume.* New York: Wiley.

Americans with Disabilities Act of 1990, 42 U.S.C.A. §§ 12101-12213 (West Supp. 1990).

Bostwick, B. E. (1990). *Resume writing: A comprehensive how-to-do-it guide.* (4th ed.). New York: Wiley.

CPC annual. (1990). (34th ed.). (4-year college edition.). Bethlehem, PA: College Placement Council.

Career guides best sellers (1990). *Library Journal, 115* (17): 77.

Civil Rights Act of 1964, 42 U.S.C. §§ 1981-2000h (1988).

Coxford, L. M. (1989). *Resume writing made easy.* (3rd ed.). Scottsdale, AZ: Gorsuch Scarisbrick.

Eyler, D. R. (1990). *Resumes that mean business.* New York: Random House.

Feild, H. S., & Holley, W. H. (1976). Resume preparation: An empirical study of personnel managers' perceptions. *Vocational Guidance Quarterly, 24:* 229-237.

Harcourt, J., & Krizan, A. C. (1989). A comparison of resume content preferences of Fortune 500 personnel administrators and business communication instructors. *Journal of Business Communication, 26:* 177-190.

Jackson, T. (1990). *The perfect resume.* New York: Doubleday.

Krannich, R. L., & Banis, W. J. (1990). *High impact resumes & letters.* (4th ed.). Woodbridge, VA: Impact.

Nadler, B. J. (1989). *Liberal arts power! What it is and how to sell it on your resume.* (2nd ed.). Princeton, NJ: Peterson's Guides.

Olney, R. J. (1982). How employers view resumes: 1974-1981. *Journal of College Placement, 42* (3): 64-67.

Parker, Y. (1989). *The damn good resume guide.* (New ed.). Berkeley, CA: Ten Speed Press.

Rehabilitation Act of 1973, 29 U.S.C. §§ 701-796 (1988).

Ryland, E. K., & Rosen, B. (1987). Personnel professionals' reactions to chronological and functional résumé formats. *Career Development Quarterly*, 35, 228-238.

Spinks, N., & Wells, B. (1987). Letters of application and resumes: A comparison of corporate views. *Bulletin of the Association for Business Communication*, 50 (3): 9-16.

Subject guide to Books in Print. (1990). New York: R. R. Bowker.

Swanson, D. (1991). *The resume solution.* Indianapolis, IN: JIST Works.

Uniform Guidelines on Employee Selection Procedures of 1978, 29 C.F.R. § 1607 (1990).

Career Resources
in Library Collections

Marilyn Searson Lary

SUMMARY. Because of the changing nature of the workplace, better access to career information should be more easily available to all types of workers. Public and academic libraries are being expected to provide career information to library patrons. This chapter suggests the type of materials which should be in a library's collection, as well as specific titles which are likely to be most useful to library users.

INTRODUCTION

There is a greater demand for career resource materials today than ever before. A volatile economy, increasingly technical and technologically-based jobs, the disappearance of many traditional areas of employment, and constantly growing needs in career change and career retraining all combine to increase the need for career materials. Although the response to such needs will vary from library to library, there are titles which should be available in every public and academic library.

The involvement of individual libraries with career education is probably based on several, unequal factors: the type and amount of career information available elsewhere; the amount of money available to support acquisition of career materials; the expectation of users and outside agencies that such information is available in the

Marilyn Searson Lary is the Director of the Library Resource Center at Dalton College, Dalton, GA 30720.

173

library; and the administrative commitment to provide this service. All these factors will determine the number of resources available, the staff assistance given to users, and the type of services offered.

BASIC CAREER INFORMATION TITLES

There are several standard titles for career information which should be in every reference collection. They contain general information on jobs, such as the characteristics of the work environment, skills and knowledge needed to fill the position successfully, and formal education/training required. Some sources will indicate occupational or industry outlook, good for those attempting to identify new or developing career options.

Perhaps the most often mentioned source, of which everyone should be aware, is the *Dictionary of Occupational Titles* (1991). The revised fourth edition lists about 20,000 occupations, providing standardized job descriptions. Indexed alphabetically by occupation and industry group, the D.O.T. covers a wide variety of occupations. A companion volume, *Selected Characteristics of Occupations Defined in the Dictionary of Occupational Titles* (1981) concentrates on providing more details on the physical demands of the occupations, their environmental conditions and the training needed for certain jobs. This source provides standard industry codes (S.I.C.) that may not be readily available in other sources. It is not critical to obtain this accompanying volume, though the information is valuable.

Another beneficial government publication is the *Occupational Outlook Handbook* (1990). Rather than a listing of occupations with brief descriptions, the *Occupational Outlook Handbook* gives prose descriptions on the nature of the work of each occupation, the qualifications needed, the earnings and working conditions, and entrance requirements for the occupations listed. Sources of additional information are listed. It is easily used by most job seekers, and its language is clear and straight-forward. This title is necessary for all libraries, for it provides basic, useful information about general occupational groups. (For anyone who may wish to manipulate the data provided in this publication, it is possible to get the historical and projected data on diskettes from the Bureau of Labor Statistics for $38.00 per disk.) The *Handbook* is updated by the periodical, *Occupational Outlook Quarterly*. This quarterly provides a great variety of employment information, from descriptions of various jobs, salaries and advancement, to articles on job searching methods and upcoming careers, to projections of employment in specific industries. It is aimed toward the professional worker.

The newly revised *Encyclopedia of Careers and Vocational Guidance* (1991), now in its eighth edition, is a four volume work which provides a gamut of information for the user. It is an invaluable source for any library. Volume one provides a six to eight page profile of more than seventy industries. Occupations in these industries are identified, and reference is made when additional information is found in the other volumes. There is an appendix of training for disabled workers and a listing of internships, apprenticeships and special training programs. At the end of each article, codes for the SIC (Standard Industrial Classification), SOC (Standard Occupational Cluster) and GOE (Guide for Occupational Exploration) are listed. There is, also, an index of DOT (Dictionary of Occupational Titles) codes for use with government publications. Association and industry contacts are provided at the end of each article. This information defines educational requirements, identifies areas for employment, and provides organizations, associations, and references which offer additional information about job opportunities. The second volume of the Encyclopedia provides information on professional careers; volume three on special and general careers; and volume four on technicians' careers. Each occupation is defined, placed in an historical context, described by the nature of the work within it, identified by the background one needs to acquire, and is further developed with information on opportunities for advancement, employment outlook, earnings, working conditions and social-psychological factors.

The *Career Information Center* (1990) is a thirteen volume set of extensive career information. Each of the first twelve volumes provide basic career information arranged by an occupational area. Similar to other career information, CIC provides data on training, salary, and the employment outlook for each profiled career. More than 3,000 jobs are discussed. Each volume provides a directory of accredited vocational training programs. Volume thirteen deals with employment trends for the upcoming decade and contains an index to the entire set. This source is easily used, and is appropriate for all who have career concerns. It is fairly expensive for a single purchase and should not be selected in lieu of any of the above noted titles.

SOURCES OF EMPLOYMENT OPPORTUNITIES

Assuming that a career choice has been made, or at least a general career area has been defined, patrons now need to find possible positions which they might enter. One time-honored method of entering a career field is through that of an internship. Although internship opportunities are sometimes built into professional programs within a college/university, other types of internships may be difficult to identify. One source that provides help in this area is *The National Directory of Internships* (1989). It describes more than 28,000 internships which cover 61 fields, including business, government and nonprofit organizations. There are three indexes which offer listings by sponsors, geographic locations, and fields. This source will undoubtedly be of greatest use in undergraduate libraries.

The College Placement Council's *CPC Annual: A Guide to Employment Opportunities for College Graduates* (1991/92) consists of several volumes devoted to employment opportunities in various fields. Each volume provides general information on employers in specific fields: type of positions, benefits, contact office, etc. For example, there is a volume devoted to health careers and one devoted to engineering and technical fields. Volume 1 and Volume 1A discuss career planning for the four-year college and the two-year college, respectively.

The Dun and Bradstreet's *The Career Guide, Dun's Employment Opportunities Directory* (1991) lists professional employment opportunities all over the United States in such areas as business, engineering, banking, health care, government–including local government, universities, technical employers, and hospitals. Each company is given detailed coverage, including areas of study which are sought, an overview of the company, career opportunities, and

methods for filling vacancies–internal promotions, college interviewing, etc. Descriptions are provided for training opportunities,
as well as career development options. State and regional locations
of the company are provided. There are indices for both the numeri-
cal and alphabetical arrangement of the Standard Industrial Classification Codes. Included are indices of employers alphabetically,
geographically and by industry. Any special benefits, such as day-
care facilities on site, are enumerated. This is a comprehensive
source which is current but expensive.

Other areas of employment which may not immediately occur to
job seekers are positions in the nonprofit sector. For descriptions of
individual careers and personal essays by individuals in specific
careers, consult the title *Careers for Dreamers and Doers: A Guide
to Management Careers in the Nonprofit Sector* (1989). This title
should be included in every library collection. Another recent edition which addresses similar positions is *Great Careers: The Fourth
of July Guide to Careers, Internships, and Volunteer Opportunities
in the Nonprofit Sector* (1990). This title describes organizations
and includes essays on careers in nonprofit organizations. It identifies professional associations, periodicals in individual fields, and
contains a bibliography of books and directories. Volunteer agencies
such as ones that fight hunger and homelessness are included.

The Jobs Rated Almanac (1988) indicates in its subtitle that it
"ranks the best & worst jobs by more than a dozen vital criteria–including salary, stress, benefits, travel and more." This almanac
covers various factors for 250 jobs. The jobs are ranked by environmental scores, male/female ratios, minority hiring, length of the
work week, income, indoor/outdoor jobs, job outlook scores, physical demands, security, geography, etc. The almanac, also, lists jobs
for those with little or no education, and comments on their prospects. *The Jobs Rated Almanac* contains a wealth of information
about the many phases and concerns of employees.

SOURCES OF CURRENTLY VACANT POSITIONS

Sources for vacant positions are, frankly, luxuries for most library collections. They will, however, enhance career resource
offerings and encourage more use of the materials. *The Career*

Opportunity Update is a monthly publication which lists hundreds of jobs in industry and government: professional, managerial, technical and clerical. Most of these positions demand experience and are primarily aimed at engineering and computer professionals. There is a "spotlight" article devoted to a specific company in each issue. Other articles provide information in various areas: surveys of salaries in particular fields, possible questions that employers may ask in an interview, and sample cover letters.

U.S. Employment Opportunities is a loose-leaf periodical that covers eighteen major industry careers in areas such as telecommunications, management consulting, art/music/dance, and the federal government. For each section, this resource provides an overview of the industry, identification of where opportunities are best, and particular resources available for that industry. Specific data contained in this publication are an identification of occupational trends, training opportunities, internships, and job-finding services.

Another title which identifies current positions is the *National Business Employment Weekly*. Taking advertisements which have appeared in the four regional issues of *The Wall Street Journal*, positions with American and foreign companies are identified in the professional, managerial, and technical areas. The positions, as a rule, require experience, and salaries range from $25,000 to $250,000. Each issue contains career advice, as well as a special section, "Talent for Hire," where individuals can advertise themselves. Twice a year there is a college supplement entitled "Managing Your Career." This is directed toward new graduates and contains advice about beginning one's career.

For those who may be interested in federal employment, there is a bi-weekly listing of professional and semi-professional vacancies in governmental agencies within this country and abroad. *Federal Career Opportunities* provides a description for each of the 3,500 jobs available, as well as application information. Advice is included on governmental policies and procedures, including tips on the development of job-seeking skills. Every three months, the open civil service registers are identified. An individual need not subscribe for an extended period of time; one can get six bi-weekly issues for a fraction of the annual subscription price of $146.00.

Publications directed toward specific groups are available. Equal Opportunity Publications of Greenlawn, New York, publishes, among others, *Careers and the Handicapped*. This publication contains a braille section and a record sound sheet bound in each issue that provides job information for those who cannot read a printed classified advertisement. Another source of positions for those in protected classes is the *Affirmative Action Register*.

Concentrating on another particular type of employment is a monthly publication, *Work Abroad*. *Work Abroad* is devoted to identifying jobs with English speaking employers: schools, hospitals, companies and other institutions abroad. It lists all types of jobs, but usually contains those which are seeking experienced professionals. The person to contact and the organization are given. This source identifies a large number of teaching positions. It is possible to obtain an individual copy of *Work Abroad* for $5.00.

COMPUTERIZED CAREER INFORMATION

One of the most obvious methods to use in providing career information is that of a computerized database. Usually, the expense of such a resource, and sometimes the need for supporting staff, eliminate this choice from most library budgets. Under most circumstances, it will require the library to be a site of state-supported career materials before a computerized career information delivery system will be available. Nevertheless, library staff should be aware of the location of such systems, for effective use of them can provide good career direction.

There are, of course, a growing number of databases of college information and career descriptions available on CD-ROM based products. One example of this is Peterson's College Database which contains the same information that is found in Peterson's annual guides to undergraduate study, *Guide to Four-Year Colleges* and *Guide to Two-Year Colleges*. The disk is available from Silver Platter for $595.00.

CAREER/OCCUPATION FACILITIES

University Facilities

There are two university career centers which deserve special mention. Both are fee-based centers which are open to the public

and operated by state-supported universities. UCLA's Career Counseling Center is administratively connected to UCLA's Extension
Division and, thus, is in a unique position to serve the community.
For a fee, the Center will provide career counseling services to an
individual. The UCLA center is strong on psychological testing in
an effort to identify careers and occupations that compare with
abilities, as well as psychological attributes. Georgia State University's Counseling Center, also, serves nonstudents. It is a fee-based
service with a staff of counseling psychologists to guide the career
seeker.

State Facilities

Almost every state has some type of employment center that
provides microfiche, computer databases, or print sources which list
state-wide positions. In addition, those who need daily workers
often visit or advertise positions in these centers. The Michigan
Occupational Information System, the largest in the United States,
is available in schools, libraries, correctional facilities, and labor
unions throughout the state. Other examples of such centers are the
Maine Career Information Delivery System and the Virginia Career
Information Delivery System.

Commercial Facilities

In addition to state-supported career facilities and those provided
by colleges and universities there are, of course, commercial enterprises which provide career evaluation and direction. Librarians
need to know of the existence of such locally available businesses
in order to make patrons aware of their availability. A direct referral
to a fee-based facility is probably unwise.

There is a unique venture that all career resources-minded folks
should monitor. With the endorsement of the College Placement
Council, a commercial effort to respond to the need for career information was begun on May 4, 1987, in Omaha, Nebraska. It was
then that Career Centers, Inc. (CCI) first began operating. Career
Centers, Inc. offers ". . . career planning assistance, occupational
information, employer literature, job-search skills training, work-

shops and seminars, a job opportunity bulletin, and a computerized resume listing and selection system.'' In addition to the endorsement of College Placement Council, it uses the CPC name and logo. Responding to local college needs, CCI offers career planning and placement services, as well as job-search workshops, to local small colleges which, otherwise, could not offer such opportunities to students and/or job-seeking alums. CCI has various services for its employer clients: interviewing skills, salary information, facilities for interviewing, and evaluating job applicants. Services are provided on a flexible fee basis, so that individuals may choose services especially appropriate for their individual needs. While CCI is not an employment agency nor a recruiting agency, it prepares employees to enter and compete successfully in obtaining positions, and it guides employers in identifying and attracting employees.

ADDITIONAL SOURCES OF INFORMATION

In addition to general materials on careers and the characteristics of particular positions, the library may need to include actual accounts of those employed in specific occupations, i.e., an art teacher, a biomedical engineer, a security guard, or a vending machine operator. Specific occupational information will more clearly describe job responsibilities, training, rewards, etc., than a generic description provided in a weighty tome. There are many producers of career information:

- Chronicle Guidance Publications, P. O. Box 1190, Moravia, NY 13118;
- Careers, Inc., Box 135, Largo, FL 34294;
- Vocational Biographies, Inc., Box 31, Sauk Center, MN 56378;
- Rosen Publishing Group, Inc., 29 E. 21st St., New York, NY 10010.

These companies produce clear descriptions of career information on a regular basis.

There are a plethora of publishers of career and job information. To evaluate their materials without "hands-on" examination, librarians need to rely on respected reviewing media: *Choice, The Booklist and Subscription Books Bulletin,* the "Career Media" column in the *Journal of Career Planning and Employment,* and *Career Development Quarterly,* to name some of the more important sources.

CONCLUSION

Each library that provides career information must evaluate the needs of its users. One facility may have far more requests for information comparing and contrasting the characteristics of various colleges than it does for the training requirements of industrial positions. The depth of the library offerings will be determined by client interests, employment opportunities in the service area, and by funds available to support this service. With funding being reduced everywhere, acquisition decisions are more critical than ever. Employment information itself is certainly more critical than ever. Provision of career and job information is becoming the responsibility of many public units. Retooling, changing careers, and the creation of totally new careers all promise to be a vital, daily concern for millions of Americans. Libraries must respond to this need in a far more active role than has heretofore been the case. Such a response includes provision of career guidance resources as well as an awareness of state, academic, or commercially sponsored job opportunities.

REFERENCES

Affirmative Action Register. St. Louis, MO: Warren H. Green, ed. and publ., 1974-. Monthly.

Block, Deborah Perlmutter and Joyce Ford Kinnison (1989). "A Method for rating computer-based career information delivery systems," *Measurement and Evaluation in Counseling and Development,* 21 (1): 177-187.

Career Guide, Dun's Employment Opportunities Directory (1991). Parsippany, NJ: Dun's Marketing Services. $425.00.

Career Information Center, 4th ed. (1990). Glencoe/Macmillan, $212.00.

Career Opportunity Update. Fountain Valley, Ca: Career Research Systems, Inc., 1988-. Monthly.

Careers and the Handicapped. Greenlawn, NY: Equal Opportunity Publications, 1986-. Semi-annual.

Careers for Dreamers and Doers: A Guide to Management Careers in the Non-profit Sector (1989). Lilly Cohen and Dennis R. Young, eds. New York: Foundation Center. $24.95.

Caulum, David and Roger Lambert (1985). *Guidelines for the Use of Computer-Based Career Information and Guidance Systems.* ERIC Report ED 266 391.

Collegiate Career Woman Magazine. Greenlawn, NY: Equal Opportunity Publications, 1973-. 3/year.

CPC Annual: A Guide to Employment Opportunities for College Graduates (1991-/92), 35th ed. Bethlehem, Pa: College Placement Council. Annual.

Dictionary of Occupational Titles, rev. 4th ed., 2 vols. (1991). Washington, DC: Government Printing Office.

Encyclopedia of Careers and Vocational Guidance, 4 vols. (1991). 8th ed. Ferguson Publishing. $129.95.

Federal Career Opportunities. Vienna, Va: Federal Research Service, Inc., 1974-. Bi-weekly.

Great Careers: the Fourth of July Guide to Careers, Internships, and Volunteer Opportunities in the Nonprofit Sector (1990). Devon Smith, ed. Garrett Park, MD: Garrett Park Press. $35.00.

Jobs Rated Almanac (1988). Les Krantz, ed. New York: Pharos Books. $14.95.

National Business Employment Weekly. Chicopee, MA: Wall Street Journal, 1987-. Weekly.

National Directory of Internships, 7th ed. (1989). National Society for Internships & Experimental Education. $22.00.

Occupational Outlook Handbook, 1990/91 (1990). Washington, DC: Government Printing Office. Biennial.

Occupational Outlook Quarterly. Washington, DC: Government Printing Office, 1957-. Quarterly.

U. S. Employment Opportunities. Arlington, VA: Washington Research Associates, 1985-. Quarterly.

Work Abroad. Ganges, British Columbia: Career Opportunities Research Center, 1984-. Monthly.

Yost, Alan E. (1988). "More than Just Another Small Business," *Journal of Career Planning and Employment,* 48 (2) 37-41.